FOAL

IN DEFENSE OF RELIGIOUS MODERATION

IN DEFENSE OF
RELIGIOUS
MODERATION

William Egginton

 Columbia University Press   New York

Columbia University Press
Publishers Since 1893
New York   Chichester, West Sussex
Copyright © 2011 William Egginton

Library of Congress Cataloging-in-Publication Data
Egginton, William, 1969–
In defense of religious moderation / William Egginton.
p. cm.
Includes bibliographical references and index.
ISBN 978-0-231-14878-8 (cloth : alk. paper) —
ISBN 978-0-231-52096-6 (ebook)
1. Religions—Relations. 2. Religious pluralism.
3. Moderation—Religious aspects. 4. Faith. I. Title

BL410.E34   2011
201'.5—dc22   2010040793

Columbia University Press books are printed on
permanent and durable acid-free paper.
This book is printed on paper with recycled content.

Printed in the United States of America

c 10 9 8 7 6 5 4 3 2 1

References to Internet Web sites (URLs) were accurate
at the time of writing. Neither the author nor Columbia
University Press is responsible for URLs that may have
expired or changed since the manuscript was prepared.

Contents

Acknowledgments (and Apologies)

The idea for this book came to me when I accepted an invitation by Sepp Gumbrecht, Andreas Kablitz, Joachim Küpper, and Stephen Nichols to speak at a colloquium at Stanford; I later presented a revised paper to the same group in Venice, so thanks are first owed to them. I am also grateful to Robert Davidson and Antonio Gómez for their kind invitations to present portions of this work at the University of Toronto and at Dartmouth College. Since then, many friends and colleagues read and commented on portions of the book's manuscript, responded to my blog posts, or suggested further readings. For such help thanks are owed to David Glass, José María García Rodríguez, Kevin Heller, Julius Morche, Marcelo Gleiser, Gianni Vattimo, Jeffrey Robbins, Serge Ugarte, Adina Roskies, Steven Peck, Steven Gross, Amy Nutt, Jim Willse, and Santiago Zabala. Thanks also to Manuel Cruz, who commissioned a summary article to publish in Spain. I also want to thank my agents Jill Kneerim and Gerald Gross for believing in the project despite those who felt it was too philosophical, or too popular, or just too moderate to sell well. Thanks to my editor, Wendy Lochner, and to Justine Evans, both at Columbia University Press. Some parts of chapter 2 are drawn from my articles "The Desire for Limitless Change," in *Reality Made Over: The Culture of Reality Television Makeover Shows* (special issue of *Configurations* 15, no. 2 [2008]: 177–91), "Danger in Legislation Based on 'Higher' Law" (op-ed piece in the *Newark Star-Ledger*, January 29, 2007), and "The Baroque as a Problem of Thought" (*PMLA* 124, no. 1 [2009]: 143–49), as well as from my book *The Theater of Truth: The Ideology of Baroque Aesthetics* (Stanford University Press, 2010). I thank the publishers for permission to reprint those passages here. Finally, it was only after finishing the book that I realized that the term "code of codes," so prevalent in its pages, had been coined by my friend and mentor Richard Rorty and must have lodged in my memory years ago only to come back as I conceived of this book. It is thus as a tribute to his influence that I use it here.

Writing a book like this has been an unfamiliar experience. My scholarly colleagues are likely to chafe at its breeziness and at my pretension of taking on a topic this vast in so few pages (and with no footnotes!). And yet despite these concessions in the hopes of wider popular consumption, it is possible that some readers will find my arguments too dense and the positions I defend counterintuitive. While the scholarship on the topics touched on in this book is almost boundless, I have had to limit references to a selected bibliography comprising those texts I've actually cited and a few others that I found indispensable for some insight they revealed or for how they changed my thinking. Naturally, this means I've neglected far more valuable sources than I've mentioned, for which I can only express the deepest regret.

This book is dedicated to the memory of my mother-in-law, Elisabeth Wegenstein.

Introduction: An Uncertain Faith

On a Wednesday morning in February 2002, a train was pulling out of the station in Godhra, in the western Indian state of Gujarat, when it was attacked by an enraged mob who pelted the compartments with stones and finally set the train on fire. Fifty-eight people, including more than a dozen children, were burned alive that morning. The reason for their excruciating deaths was that they were Hindus traveling through a part of India with a large Muslim population. They were, moreover, members of a group, the World Hindu Council, that had been organizing the construction of a temple on the site of a previously razed mosque. The mob that attacked the train was composed of Muslims.

Atrocities such as this one provoke a sense of outrage among Americans who read about them in the papers or see news reports on CNN. Western reporters attribute the violence and mayhem to "religious extremists" or to "religious conflict" between Hindu and Muslim "fundamentalists," and eventually these acts become fodder for critics who argue passionately that religion—as the title of Christopher Hitchens's popular book puts it—poisons everything. Indeed, it is hard not to be persuaded by this argument when we are confronted by the litany of violence, abuse, humiliation, and pain that religious people of all affiliations have inflicted on others, apparently since the dawn of recorded history.

According to today's critics, while some believers are more prone to violence than others, essentially religion itself is to blame. As the comedian and outspoken atheist Bill Maher has put it, there is no difference between being religious and being an extremist, because "if your beliefs are extreme, you're an extremist." For these critics, a religious moderate is simply someone whose commitment to his faith is not as deeply felt as that of a religious fundamentalist. His or her beliefs are as extreme, but they are just watered down for easier public consumption. Even worse, by endorsing a mellower version of essentially extreme beliefs, these moderates help spread the noxious creeds that the extremists ultimately act on.

But what if this analysis gets it exactly wrong? What if religious belief is not the reason that the Muslim mob burned the Hindu activists? What if religious belief is not the reason that Christian crusaders slaughtered Muslims in the Middle Ages, that Catholics tortured Protestants during the Counterreformation, that Muslims flew themselves into skyscrapers in 2001? At first blush, the idea seems absurd. Of course religious belief was the cause of all these acts! What else could it have been?

What I argue in this book is that in every case where "religious fundamentalists" have been guilty of committing atrocities, the *religious* part of that moniker is incidental. What drives people to otherwise unimaginable acts of violence is not religion at all, it is *fundamentalism*, and *fundamentalism has no more to do with religion than with any other possible kind of belief.* Moreover, a certain kind of religious belief, what I call in this book religious moderation, is not only innocent of the charges that critics have brought against religion *but also the best possible defense against the dangers that fundamentalism poses to just and peaceful societies.*

The key to this claim is the concept of faith. For religion's critics, faith means merely "belief without evidence." The critics point out that when we accept certain beliefs without evidence, as adherents to any religious faith must do, there is no way to prove us wrong. Therefore, when we are told that God wants us to build a temple in exactly the place where adherents to a different faith have their temple, our only option is to

believe that we are right, that they are wrong, and that their opposition
to our plan is the only obstacle blocking us from fulfilling God's will.
That this is an automatic recipe for violent conflict seems hard to deny.

But what the critics either do not understand or purposefully
obscure is that, for many religious people, the way they live their
faith doesn't at all correspond to "belief without evidence." For these
religious moderates, the more appropriate definition of faith would
be something like "belief in something about which there can be no
evidence." The critics might well accuse me of nitpicking here, but
the distinction is actually of enormous importance, because what
separates religious moderates from religious fundamentalists is not
so much *what* they believe, the religious part, as *how* they believe.
Fundamentalists see only a difference of degree between belief and
knowledge, belief being a kind of provisional version of knowledge.
For moderates, in contrast, human knowledge is essentially incapable
of grasping everything, and, as a result, there are and must be some
things we *believe* without ever possibly coming to *know* them.

When we believe something in a moderate, as opposed to a fundamentalist, way, we tend to think of it as subject to contestation, to
correction by further or better knowledge, to discussion and interpretation. When we believe something in a fundamentalist way, in
contrast, we think of it as ultimate and unchanging, never subject to
further interpretation or discussion.

One way of picturing the difference between these ways of believing is to imagine a group of children playing a game in which they
sit blindfolded in a circle and try to describe an object. If one of them
secretly takes off his blindfold and sees exactly what the object is, he
now *knows* what the others can only *think* or *believe* is there. While the
others argue back and forth about which interpretation is better, the
cheating child no longer needs to take part in the discussion.

Now let's project the circumstances of this simple game onto the
entirety of human knowledge. While someone may take the blindfold
off when dealing with an object in a room, there is no such thing as
seeing the whole of the universe as it really is apart from our different
attempts to measure and explain it, or as understanding the ultimate
meaning of life apart from its various interpretations. This is the case
because seeing and understanding are human activities that depend

on our senses and concepts and take place over time and in space. There can be no seeing or understanding or, for that matter, any kind of knowledge that can comprehend the totality of the world as it is in itself independent of our senses, our concepts, the movement of time, or positioning in space. Just to make this last point clear: what would it mean for you to know any object or experience if you were able to look at it simultaneously from every possible perspective and from every moment in time, or if you were asked to describe it without being limited by the senses of your body or the concepts of your language?

To believe something in a fundamentalist way is to claim implicitly that you are the seeing child in a room full of blindfolded children. It is not merely believing that you know more than others; there are many cases in which you might be justified in believing that. Rather, it is believing that there is an ultimate way to know the world and that you have access to that knowledge. Since that knowledge is ultimate, it is never subject to correction, and hence anyone with even a slightly different interpretation must be wrong. If my neighbor and I each believed in this way that, for example, our own recipe for paella was the best and indeed only way to make paella, while we might refuse to eat each other's paella, the resulting conflict would not necessarily end in violence. If, however, we each happened to believe in this way that the land we communally inhabited was our own to do with as we wished, then we would likely have a serious problem.

As it turns out, a key issue in the current debate between the "new atheists" and their religious opponents concerns what happens at a cognitive level when we say we *believe* something. Sam Harris, one of the main voices of the new atheism (although, as he points out, he doesn't use the term *atheist* to describe himself) and a researcher in the field of the neuroscience of religion, based his earlier diatribes against religious belief on the explicit and unsupported claim that there is only one cognitive structure to all beliefs: that of a proposition. As he has put it, "Believing a given proposition is a matter of believing that it faithfully represents some state of the world." In other words, all beliefs correspond to the form "I believe that S is P" and thus can be evaluated as truth claims based on the availability of evidence for the claim that, indeed, S is P. In light of this position, Harris has consistently defined faith as belief without evidence.

When societies are dominated by people of faith, people who are compelled to believe unreasonable propositions about the world without evidence, the result is a recipe for intolerance, injustice, and violence.

I should interject here that this impulse to violence is, at the very least, shared by Harris. As he has said, "there is, in fact, no talking to some people. If they cannot be captured, and they often cannot, otherwise tolerant people may be justified in killing them in self-defense." The justification for such intolerance from otherwise tolerant people is that people of faith by definition fall outside a sphere of civil conversation that other, normal people, inhabit.

Now, in Harris's estimation some 240 million of the current 300 million inhabitants of the United States fall into the category of people with whom there is just no talking by virtue of their responses to surveys asking about their religious beliefs. He is also less willing to grant what fellow atheist Richard Dawkins suggests, that a good portion of those responding to such surveys don't really mean it when they say they are believers.

While I am not proposing to undermine such survey responses in the same way Dawkins does, I would contend that there is a considerable spectrum of possible meanings for the claim to believe that is attributable to so many U.S. citizens. The mere fact that a majority of U.S. Catholics fail to follow the Church's teaching on contraception profoundly undermines this conception of implicit unanimity in the way believers believe. More recent research in the neurology of religious belief, including articles coauthored by Harris, has demonstrated perceptible differences in brain activity between religious and nonreligious test subjects, and research conducted by Andrew Newberg and others has revealed different regions of activity in the brain in the same subject when that subject focuses on religious as opposed to nonreligious thought contents.

The conclusion to draw from this should be quite clear: we have no justification at all, and indeed much evidence to the contrary, that all beliefs share the same cognitive structure. But if this is true, then the entire justification for the attack on all religious beliefs as if they were coresponsible for the evils of fundamentalism (a core point of agreement among the new atheists) simply vanishes. In fact, it may well be that various forms of nonfundamentalist or moderate religious belief are far more subversive of fundamentalist thinking than all the bombast and aggression the new atheists can muster.

An immediate result of seeing the problem of fundamentalism as having to do not with *what* one believes but with *how* one believes is that we can begin to grasp how all sorts of beliefs, and not just religious ones, can be affected by fundamentalist thinking. While there can be no doubt that religious beliefs, when held in a fundamentalist way, are among the most explosive, beliefs about politics, morality, and identity are equally combustible. Indeed, the major weakness of today's critics of religion is the way they have to pick and choose their examples of atrocity to ensure that religion stays front and center as society's worst ill, which leads to some entertaining feats of logical acrobatics when it comes to discussing totalitarianism (Hitchens finds himself forced to argue that the emphatically antireligious movements of German National Socialism and Soviet Stalinism were actually thinly disguised religions) and to a total silence on certain cases of ethnic violence.

While fundamentalist thinking is socially harmful in very obvious ways when applied to politics, morality, and religion, there are myriad other ways in which it can have noxious effects, which are often not nearly so obvious. For this reason, the second chapter of this book is dedicated to unearthing ways of being fundamentalist that are not usually recognized as such and that can be the cause of serious social problems. These everyday fundamentalisms are sometimes hard to see. Unlike their religious cousins, everyday fundamentalisms don't trumpet their values to the world; instead, they work surreptitiously to color the way we think about our roles in the world and our relations with other people and thus exert a powerful sway on our culture, politics, and personal lives.

I listed two central claims for this book: if the first claim is that fundamentalism is a separate phenomenon from religion and that it and not religion is to blame for many of the worst social ills, the second claim is that there is a kind of religious belief that is not only *not* in cahoots with fundamentalism but also really the best defense against it. This sort of belief is what I am calling religious moderation.

Recall that what is specific about fundamentalist thinking is that it recognizes no aspect of existence that is out of bounds of human knowledge; as long as you are one of the chosen or have adopted the right interpretive framework, everything about existence is ultimately knowable. In other words, for the fundamentalist everything we could ever seek to know, the totality of the universe, already exists as a kind of knowledge. This knowledge can be thought of as a sort of master code underlying everything that we perceive, much like the giant computer program that created the world-sized virtual reality in the movie *The Matrix*. Once we accept that everything we see, feel, or otherwise experience is merely an expression of that fundamental *code of codes*, our task is merely to learn how to read it.

This is an extremely appealing notion, and not only for the religiously inclined. Indeed, the idea of the world as the expression of a hidden master code has a long history and has had as much nourishment from the defenders of science as it has from the explicitly religious. There are some kinds of belief, though, that explicitly distrust and undermine this fundamentalist notion of an all-encompassing code of codes; one of them is the theological tradition that has dovetailed with the history of religious fundamentalism and has often served to temper its absolutism and criticize its pretensions. The different forms of moderate religious belief that have emerged from institutions with long histories of theological inquiry thus have the potential of not merely tempering religious fanaticism but also undermining the basic impulses behind all fundamentalist thinking.

The key theological insight that is most damaging to the fundamentalist attitude is that the very idea of the code of codes, the core of any and all fundamentalism, is impossible. While the theological tradition of religious moderation obviously does not deny God's existence, such theologies are unified in insisting on God's essentially ineffable nature. That is to say, if God exists, his "knowledge" of the world would have to be equivalent to the way the world is in itself, independent of human knowledge. But such knowledge would be utterly incompatible with human knowledge, which can grasp the world only through senses and concepts, over time and situated in space. What this means is emphatically not that the world as it is in itself does not exist but that it does not exist *as knowledge*, that there is not and cannot be a code of codes underlying all existence. By continually insisting on the impossibility of any such total and ultimate knowledge, religious moderation unhinges the very foundation of fundamentalist thinking on all fronts, religious or otherwise.

Accordingly, the third chapter explores the history of fundamentalism as the expression of a hidden code of codes and shows how that fundamentalist thinking got smuggled into the ostensibly secular modern European worldview informing present-day U.S. society. Simultaneously, however, I also show how the history of religious thought contains numerous instances of theology that undermines and openly criticizes the assumptions of fundamentalism. The obvious lesson to glean from these histories is that moderate theology is the baby swimming around in the dirty bathwater of religious ideology, and if we empty it out we risk losing a very powerful tool against fundamentalism in all its forms.

Now, aside from openly fundamentalist believers in one of the so-called religions of the book—Judaism, Christianity, and Islam—I am not suggesting that many people consciously believe that there is a code of codes; in practice, though, many people act as though they believed just that. Certainly we could understand if this were a widespread assumption among scientists otherwise disinclined to believe in metaphysical certainties. The great mathematician Sir Roger Penrose, for example, who has openly admitted to holding "to no religious doctrine," has also publicly and passionately advocated for his belief that mathematics has the value of something like a code of codes and that we should therefore be "careful to distinguish the precise mathematical entities from the approximations that we see around us in the world of physical things." But if what we see in the world of physical things are mere approximations, then the language of mathematics is telling us something about things that are not approximations, that are, in other words, things as they are in themselves.

Still, the beliefs of world-famous mathematicians like Roger Penrose should not be taken as typical of how people tend to view the world. The code of codes need not refer to a scientist's confidence in the objective truth of certain laws or principles. What is this code of codes, then, such that it makes such a difference in the way we interact with one another and the world? The code of codes is the implicit and mostly unacknowledged belief that beyond the veil of how the world appears to us, here and now, there is a deeper reality on which our lived reality is based, and, most important, this deeper reality *encodes* our own. By saying that it encodes our reality, what I mean is that, like any code, the deeper reality consists of a potentially readable set of instructions for producing the physical reality in which we live.

Belief in the code of codes is widespread, powerful, and at the heart of what we could call the religion of arrogance. Belief in the code of codes leads to arrogance because when we figure the perceived world as relying on a code, we are assuming by definition that the code can be read and, therefore, that someone can ultimately be in possession of a knowledge that could never be surpassed, never be corrected. Indeed, were it possible for humanity to finally obtain something like the code of codes, whether by religious or scientific means, the inquiries that we call science or theology, or even the stance we call faith for that matter, would cease to be relevant. Because the very notion of the code of codes requires that it be ultimate, a society in possession of it can no longer consider faith (as the decision to believe in something one cannot know), science (as the search for further knowledge), or even ethics (as the questioning of right and wrong) to be remotely useful endeavors.

Nevertheless, is there not a huge difference between a religious zealot ready to kill those who do not adhere to his doctrine and a scientist who believes that the totality of being can theoretically be known, although it is not in fact known today? While this is doubtless true, the slope spanning these two positions is slippery indeed. Although the atheist thinkers I engage with in this book are not dangerous in the same way a religious extremist most certainly is and are certainly the furthest thing from ignorant in the way that an advocate of creation science most certainly is, the aggression with which they push their agendas and the certainty with which they stake claims to metaphysical truths make them closer to their religious counterparts than they may think.

More important, the actual practice of science, the work that leads to our greater understanding of the world we live in, is never in fact engaged with decoding the totality of being; rather, it is always concerned with understanding this or that mystery as it faces us here and now. Science, in other words, is concerned with the world as it appears to us, as we inhabit it with our bodies and come to know it through our media and technologies; it is concerned with observations, measurements, and verifiable predictions. It is only when scientists philosophize (incorrectly) about what they are engaged in that they mistake their worthy endeavors for a kind of miscreant theology, replacing the task of studying aspects of the world in time and space with the pretension to know the world as it really is independent of time and space.

In the book's last chapter, I explain exactly what I mean when I say that religious moderation is the best defense against fundamentalism. To do this I begin by identifying what practices count as religious moderation and to what extent the religions people are practicing today really correspond to that definition. As it turns out, even at a time when so many decry the return of religious fundamentalism—citing statistics like Sam Harris's claim that four out of five Americans "apparently believe that Jesus will return someday and orchestrate the end of the world with his magic powers"—in fact the great majority of Americans, as well as an enormous number of people the world over, live their faiths in a moderate as opposed to a fundamentalist way. What this means is that these believers, far from believing in doctrines despite all evidence to the contrary, are embracing in practice a faith that safeguards an open, inquisitive, even scientific knowledge about the world against the noxious certainty of fundamentalist thinking. This uncertain faith not only is compatible with science, dialogue, pluralism, and the institutions underlying the democratic rule of law, but also actively works to uphold and protect those values and institutions from the encroachment of thoroughly undemocratic fundamentalisms.

In his historic inaugural address on January 20, 2009, President Barack Obama famously declared that the United States "is a country of Christians and Muslims, of Jews and Hindus, and of nonbelievers." What Obama was signaling with these words was the importance to its democracy of America's tradition of religious pluralism, a tradition the philosopher Martha Nussbaum has also recently defended in her book *Liberty of Conscience*. In that book she presents a purely philosophical defense of religious toleration while at the same time locating herself, an observant Reform Jew, in a particular religious tradition. Like Nussbaum's book, this one too is written from a philosophical as opposed to a religious perspective. I do not rely on a single assumption in its pages that would not be acceptable to anyone willing to engage in rational discussion without prejudice or bias, and though I defend a certain kind of religious belief on philosophical grounds, I certainly do not base that defense on the doctrine of any particular religion.

To come back to the president's declaration, it is important that, along with four major religions, he included the category of nonbelievers. The current debate about religion has been dominated by a group of writers whose vitriol against all religion is matched only by the passion of their own nonbelief. While my philosophical arguments find religious moderation to be a better defense than atheism against the ills of fundamentalism, it is vital to add that the values of moderation hold for this argumentation as well. Insofar as an atheist is willing to consider his or her nonbelief in God as a belief and not a doctrine of certainty, and there is plenty of evidence that many of them are, then it seems to me that his or her belief fits every bit as well into my notion of moderation as do the more specifically religious practices I point to. Ultimately, such atheists join with religious moderates in insisting that human knowledge is essentially limited and partial. Such atheists join religious moderates in rejecting any philosophy, ideology, or religion that claims to have certainty about the ultimate nature of the universe or the ultimate meaning of life, and instead they acknowledge how profoundly reasonable it is that humans have some beliefs that are themselves not founded on reason. Because the realm of what we believe will always, inevitably, be greater in extent and ambition than the realm of what we know, how much wiser it is to protect what we can know from the clutches of errant beliefs by marking off a territory in our lives for belief without knowledge! Far from assaulting the sacred precinct of science, religious moderation safeguards scientific progress, the trial and error of democracy, and the mutual edification of pluralism, and does so by giving the sacred a precinct of its own, freed from the arrogance of certainty by the humility of an uncertain faith.

IN DEFENSE OF RELIGIOUS MODERATION

1 Dogmatic Atheism

The Complexity of Belief

Bill Maher's highly successful and often hilarious documentary *Religulous* ends with the comedian summing up his views on religion against a background of images of violence, death, and destruction. This sequence is nothing short of a call to arms, addressed to "rational people" and "antireligionists," to end their timidity, come out of the closet, and assert themselves. His terms, as one might put it, are nonnegotiable, and his list of judgments includes

- It's a plain fact, religion must die if mankind is to live.
- Faith means making a virtue out of not thinking.
- Those who preach faith, and enable and elevate it, are our intellectual slaveholders.
- Those who consider themselves only moderately religious have to look in the mirror and realize that the solace and comfort that religion brings you actually comes at a terrible price.

And the last words of the film: "That's it. Grow up, or die."

Linked to such frightening images, including the obligatory final mushroom cloud, and spliced with snippets from interviews with fanatics overlaid with appropriately apocalyptic quotations from the various scriptures, the film's final turn from humorous critic of religious creeds and their adherents to harbinger of doom reveals a sleight of hand present in the writings of all those associated with what has been called the new atheism. By making the evils they catalog the result of faith instead of fanaticism, the critics hold a group of people in principle opposed to violence accountable for atrocities of the most barbaric kind.

Maher waxes philosophical during this sequence, and in so doing he touches on the real problem. "Religion," he says, "is dangerous because it allows human beings who don't have all the answers to think that they do. . . . The only appropriate attitude for man to have about the big questions is not the arrogant certitude that is the hallmark of religion, but doubt. Doubt is humble, and that's what man needs to be, considering that human history is just a litany of getting shit dead wrong."

This is, of course, an admirable position; in fact, it is exactly the position I am advocating in this book. The only difference is that while I am attributing it to religious and other moderates, Maher and the new atheists assume that all believers lack it to the same degree and that only they and their fellow antireligionists are deserving of the epithet of doubter. But aside from the occasional afterthought, a kind of window dressing of doubt to clear them of the ever-threatening charge of their own private fundamentalism, the new atheists' rhetoric is almost entirely devoid of any real doubt as to the ultimate truth of their position and is on the contrary almost bursting with a contempt for religious beliefs fed by their absolute certainty that those beliefs are, without exception, false.

There are two unfounded assumptions, then, at the heart of the atheist challenge: first, that faith is incompatible with doubt and, second, that there can be certainty about the falsity of religious claims. But far from being an obvious antagonist to faith, as I show in the third chapter, moderate religious practice as well as much of the theological tradition have placed doubt at the very heart of faith. When Philip Seymour Hoffman's troubled priest says about doubt, in John Patrick Shanley's film of the same name, that it "can be a bond as powerful as certainty," he is echoing the opinion of religious thinkers from Saint Thomas Aquinas to Paul Tillich. As far as the second assumption is concerned, that there can be certainty about the falsity of religious claims, the entire weight of the distinction between atheism and agnosticism falls on it. To the extent that the critics in question soften their position and embrace doubt on "the big questions," as Maher puts it, then we are in the same camp. But they cannot do so with any consistency, since the marketability of their product depends on the vehemence of their attack. Atheists thus have to feign certainty where there can be none, and in order to do that, they must distort another common notion such that it becomes almost unrecognizable. That notion is belief.

Sam Harris dedicates a chapter early on in his book *The End of Faith* to the problem of belief. From his perspective, belief is a problem only when religion's defenders claim a different status for religious beliefs than for beliefs about how things are in the world. For Harris, in contrast, "believing a given proposition is a matter of believing that it faithfully represents some state of the world." Any other kind of belief simply does not make sense. This is an important assumption for Harris to make because it and it alone guarantees that the ills he chalks up to religious belief are attributable to all believers, even those who reject a literal interpretation of scripture. By discounting the enormous middle ground of people who count themselves as believers without thereby actually believing that the world was made in six days about six thousand years ago, Harris can group them all together into a camp of the ultimately unreasonable, of those who believe absurd things without evidence and are thus outside the boundaries of reasonable discourse, those about whom he says, "There is, in fact, no talking to some people. If they cannot be captured, and they often cannot, otherwise tolerant people may be justified in killing them in self-defense."

As is apparent from this last sentence, a lot lies on this assumption. Harris is merely making explicit the threat of violence behind this reduction of all belief to one, propositional kind. Once we assume that all stated beliefs are, as Harris puts it, "processes by which our understanding (and *mis*understanding) of the world is represented and made available to guide our behavior" and that they are, furthermore, either true or false representations of the world, with nothing in between, then the recourse to violence indeed seems inevitable.

But both assumptions are, in fact, false. Beliefs are far more varied and complex than Harris assumes and, because they are not merely in a representational relation to the world, are not divided exclusively into true and false ones.

What do we mean when we say we believe something? Well, as becomes quickly apparent, that depends a lot on what we are saying we believe. Try answering these yes/no questions without spending a lot of time on them:

- Do you believe it is raining outside?
- Do you believe it will rain tomorrow?
- Do you believe that the sum of the squares of a right triangle's two shortest sides is equal to the square of its hypotenuse?
- Do you believe smoking is bad for your health?
- Do you believe smoking is enjoyable?
- Do you believe you are happily married?
- Do you believe your best friend is happily married?
- Do you believe in love at first sight?
- Do you believe in Santa Claus?
- Do you believe Mozart's music was divinely inspired?
- Do you believe that William Shakespeare wrote *Hamlet*?
- Do you believe that Hamlet's uncle killed Hamlet's father?
- Do you believe in God?

Clearly, I could go on for a long time, but this is probably enough to illustrate my point. Harris, who did a doctorate in neuroscience at UCLA focusing on the neurology of belief, disbelief, and uncertainty (and therefore, one hopes, knows something about it) writes that, "at present, we have no understanding of what it means, at the level of the brain, to say that a person believes or disbelieves a given proposition." Yet despite this admission of ignorance he was certain enough to base two books and numerous articles and speeches attacking religious belief on the undemonstrated assumption that we all understand precisely the same thing each time we read the word *believe* in the questions above.

It is not at all clear, however, that this is the case. Philosopher and cognitive scientist Kenneth Sayre, for instance, has identified at least four different types of cognitive attitudes determining a belief's conceptual environment and, hence, how it ultimately functions at a cognitive level. As I mentioned, recent research in the neurosciences, including work by Harris, has shown that religious and nonreligious test subjects register perceptible differences in brain activity; and research conducted by Andrew Newberg and others has shown that the same subject can register different brain activity when he or she focuses on religious as opposed to nonreligious thought contents. Given this variety it is certainly plausible that the statistics Harris enjoys quoting concerning 240 million Americans who believe in the imminence of the Second Coming may not mean exactly what Harris says they mean when they use the word *believe*. And I don't mean, as Richard Dawkins has suggested, that people are consciously misrepresenting their beliefs when they answer surveys because they want to appear religious or convince themselves that they believe things they in fact don't. As simple a question as "Do you believe in God?" may in some respondents involve completely different cognitive functions than does the question "Do you believe it is raining now?" The point is, we don't know. And yet the entire weight of the atheist attack on religion requires that we do know.

I would argue, in fact, that it is much more reasonable to assume that when people answer different questions concerning their beliefs they are using the word in different ways and with markedly different presuppositions. When someone answers a question about belief concerning something he or she perceives at that moment, about something he or she can speculate will occur, about a character in a work of fiction, about an aesthetic value judgment, or about belief in a metaphysical being, not only is it very likely that term will have different meanings in each context but it is also probable that different people will use the term differently when answering the same question.

My claim is that the kind of people I am calling religious moderates mean something very different when they say they believe in God than do religious fundamentalists when they say that they believe in God and than do atheists when they say they do not believe in God. The difference is that atheists and fundamentalists believe either explicitly or implicitly that the ultimate reality they are referring to when they speak about the existence or nonexistence of God is knowable and in fact already formulated as knowledge—a secret language encoding every appearance in the universe. Their sentences about the ultimate nature of the universe, then, are either true or false. As Harris has expressed it, "Either the Bible is just an ordinary book, written by mortals, or it isn't. Either Christ was divine, or he was not."

Harris writes these lines, incidentally, in a moment of unrestrained camaraderie with fundamentalists, having just identified religious moderates as his and their common enemy: "Of course, there are Christians who do not agree with either of us. There are Christians who consider other faiths to be equally valid paths to salvation." Against these religious moderates, Harris enjoins his fundamentalist brethren to "observe that the issue is both simpler and more urgent than liberals and moderates generally admit." Indeed, simple and urgent is exactly how fundamentalists see issues, which is why they are quick to provoke, quick to find enemies, and quick to take up arms when the occasion presents itself, often long before peaceful means of conflict resolution have been explored.

Certain beliefs are, indeed, either true or false. It will be the case that it is or it is not raining outside, regardless of what you believe is the case. It is also the case that the sum of the squares of a triangle's two shortest sides is equal to the square of its hypotenuse, again regardless of what you believe. Belief in the existence of God is an example of a category of beliefs that neither have such a relation to a verifiable sensory experience nor are what philosophers call a priori truths, statements that are true without having to be experientially verified. Such metaphysical beliefs are, in Karl Popper's terminology, nonfalsifiable and, while they make for very bad scientific hypotheses, they are exactly what articles of faith are about. We do not have faith in the same mundane and falsifiable way that we have beliefs about the world, and it is a mistake to think that we do.

The Science of Atheism

According to the logic of the code of codes, the job of scientific practice is to form an accurate picture of how the world in fact is. Scientific knowledge is figured as a *translation* into our terms of a code that, while perhaps partially or temporarily obscured, is fundamentally legible and compatible with human knowledge.

This logic is as ubiquitous as it is apparently immune to being dispelled or undermined; it is as common a presumption in intellectuals of the secular left as it is in moralizers of the Christian right. In the recent words of Joel Agee, memoirist and translator of, among others, Heinrich von Kleist, "To write is to translate—not from another language, but from a formless, darkly stirring source where what needs to be said is felt to be potentially or even actually present. That is how the impossible work begins. Gradually, and sometimes in bursts, the translation into language takes shape, and when it is done, it seems like a miracle."

Despite being an eloquent and stirring expression of what many may in fact experience as the act of writing, Agee's description imports exactly the fundamentalist logic I have been describing into an activity that, on closer observation, many would agree is as secular and human as it gets. The attribution of the miraculous seems almost like an afterthought; what is at issue is the notion that knowledge is a kind of translation of another language, felt to be potentially or even actually present.

If this logic is religious, then, it is religious only for the following reason: it ascribes to the unknown the quality of being knowledge; and because *someone* must have a knowledge in order for it to be knowledge, in the case where the unknown is figured as an *absolute unknown*, that someone, implicitly, is God. God speaks a language, and the language he speaks is that of a reality yet to be known, of truths yet to be unveiled.

This logic persists in the most blatantly atheistic discourses, such as that of today's most ubiquitous atheist, the former Simonyi Professorship Chair of the Public Understanding of Science at Oxford University, Richard Dawkins. Like Harris, Dawkins has very little patience for moderation or tolerance in matters of religion. In fact, agnosticism, the principled position not to claim any metaphysical knowledge, is the target of some of his harshest vituperation. In *The God Delusion* Dawkins distinguishes between two types of agnosticism, which he refers to as, respectively, TAP (temporary agnosticism in practice) and PAP (permanent agnosticism in principle):

TAP . . . is the legitimate fence-sitting where there really is a definite answer, one way or the other, but we so far lack the evidence to decide it (or don't understand the evidence, or haven't time to read the evidence, etc). TAP would be a reasonable stance towards the Permian extinction. There is a truth out there and one day we hope to know it, but for the moment we don't.

In contrast, "the PAP style of agnosticism is appropriate for questions that can never be answered no matter how much evidence we gather, because the very idea of evidence is not applicable. The question exists on a different plane, or in a different dimension, beyond the zones where evidence can reach."

Dawkins's point is that agnostics of the second type place knowledge of the existence of God into precisely such a zone of nonfalsifiability, whereas he suggests that such knowledge be treated exactly like any other knowledge: subject to eventual falsifiability or, at least and in the meantime, to judgments concerning its probability. (His conclusion: very, very unlikely.)

The problem, however, with being a merely Temporary Agnostic in Practice, at least according to Dawkins's definition, is that it necessarily implies a logic that is, paradoxically, through and through religious. Take the statement about the Permian extinction, the hypothesis that the "greatest mass extinction in fossil history" could have been caused by a "meteorite strike like the one which, with greater likelihood on present evidence, caused the later extinction of the dinosaurs." In this case the hypothesis to be proven rests in the temporal and spatial domain of human knowledge, and hence we can expect or hope to gather enough evidence about it to eventually embrace it or reject it as the truth. In the case of the existence or nonexistence of God, however, the hypothesis concerns not an aspect of phenomenal existence but the absolute entirety of space and time. In inferring from a phenomenally limited case of verifiable knowledge to the phenomenally unlimited, Dawkins smuggles in a fundamental assumption about the nature of the whole: namely, that it exists as a potential object of cognition, that, in its entirety in space and time, the universe already has the structure of being knowable, which means that it is ideally subject to description by a language and that our task is merely to translate that language.

More than simply religious, this position is specifically fundamentalist. Furthermore, there are, as will be seen in the third chapter, explicitly religious—that is, theological—inquiries that come to conclusions totally contrary to such fundamentalism. In other words, there are cases in which starting from moderately religious presuppositions leads one to positions that are less fundamentalist and more conducive to the practice of science than the one Dawkins advocates.

To be more specific, let us take the case of the so-called intelligent design movement. As a strict Darwinist, Dawkins obviously finds intelligent design—the argument that the evidence of life is better explained by reference to a creator than to random mutation and natural selection—to be a very bad idea. He would therefore be loath to admit that his own position is more closely aligned with that of intelligent design than is a rigorously applied theology of the sort worked out in the thirteenth century by Saint Thomas Aquinas—from whose cosmological proof for the existence of God the very term *intelligent design* is derived.

In fact, where Dawkins's position allows for the appearance of a reasonable debate between intelligent design theorists and Darwinians on the relative probability of their respective theories, Thomism demonstrates a priori that the science of intelligent design is based on a category mistake. The key to this argument, as Michael W. Tkacz has shown, is Aquinas's dictum that "Creatio non est mutatio" (Creation is not change). By removing creation from the very realm of discussions concerning physical change in the phenomenal world, Aquinas ensured that his own faith in the reality of God would in no way impinge on the efforts of science to discover new truths about the physical world. In other words, Aquinas used his faith in order to make room for knowledge, knowledge unencumbered by the need to speak about the totality of existence or the absolute, as his faith was already doing that in a completely different register. Dawkins, in contrast, by wanting to include hypotheses about the whole of existence in the realm of temporal and spatial knowledge, effectively grants intelligent design theorists a place at the table with evolution by natural selection, as if they were formulating hypotheses that *could be falsified*.

As a Darwinist, Dawkins might understandably feel appalled to be said to be making arguments that are compatible with intelligent design, but that is in fact what he is doing. Perhaps the most influential writer to promote the intelligent design thesis is Michael Behe. In his *Darwin's Black Box* he advances the argument that certain biological traits are irreducibly complex, meaning that it is inconceivable that they would have evolved by random mutation when no single element of the trait offers any selective advantage. Followers of intelligent design are enamored of particular cases of quite complex traits that provide obvious survival advantages but for which no single step in the evolutionary process seems to provide such an advantage on its own. A well-cited case is that of the bombardier beetle's ability to secrete enzyme catalysts that produce a microexplosion in its bowels releasing a burst of liquid at 100 degrees Celsius. From the intelligent design perspective, it is hopelessly naive to think that such an amazing mechanism evolved by chance, because, its followers assume, such complexity cannot be broken down into steps but must have emerged as an entire and already functioning trait. Given this assumption, the intelligent design supporter mocks the Darwinist, saying, "Just think how many beetles must have blown themselves up before one finally got that trick right!"—and quickly concludes that none had to because God gave the beetles this little weapon in a perfectly functioning form.

A popular author among the Christian right, Grant Jeffrey (who in addition to advocating for intelligent design theory has authored books interpreting the war in Iraq as fulfilling the prophesies of the end of days) approvingly deploys the irreducible complexity argument:

> One of the greatest problems facing those who deny a creator is to explain how natural selection or random mutation could evolve such a phenomenally complex organ as the human eye when none of the hundreds of thousands of imagined intermediate mutations could have any survival value whatever until the completed optical system was in place to allow vision to take place. The only rational conclusion is that God instantly created the fully developed human eye when He first created Adam and Eve.

Like Dawkins, proponents of intelligent design believe that the idea of creation by God should be treated in the same way as we treat the hypothesis of speciation by random mutation, but the result of this position is to block further inquiry past any assessment of irreducible complexity. Complexity is irreducible, in other words, precisely insofar as it has not been reduced by further inquiry; and creation is a perfectly good justification for the cessation of inquiry.

Dawkins—ostensibly representing the diametrically opposed position to such obscurantism—also places creation and speciation by mutation on the same level, albeit in order to subject creation to rational scrutiny. Yet by so doing he places his own enunciations concerning the ultimate nature of the cosmos on exactly the same level as the creationists place their claims, namely, that of assuming the truth of a proposition instead of allowing the space for the potentially endless inquiry into the nature of things.

The Violence of Certainty

The problem with all atheist attacks on religion today is that while they are right in decrying the evils they catalog, they are wrong in how they attribute the cause. Not only that, in most cases the critics of religion themselves are aware that religion per se is not their real target. When faced with the usual objection that secularists also commit atrocities—just witness the twentieth century—both Sam Harris and Christopher Hitchens reply that Stalinism, Nazism, and all the rest were really religions in disguise. Hitchens, for example, in his book *God Is Not Great: How Religion Poisons Everything* generalizes about the philosophical nature of totalitarianism on the basis of a curious historical genealogy, claiming that it finds it true origins in the Jesuit missions in Paraguay and ergo that "the object of perfecting the species—which is the very root and source of the totalitarian impulse—is in essence a religious one." He subsequently supports this claim with a pithy quote from his mentor-muse George Orwell, who wrote that "*a totalitarian state is in effect a theocracy*, and its ruling caste, in order to keep its position, has to be thought of as infallible."

It should be clear at once that we are witnessing a kind of three-shell game in which the ball of religion has been whisked away at just the right moment and replaced with another object altogether. This becomes all the more obvious when Hitchens tries to force the new subject—fundamentalism—back into the general category of religion: "Religion even at its meekest has to admit that what it is proposing is a 'total' solution, in which faith must be to some extent blind, and in which all aspects of the private and public life must be submitted to a permanent higher supervision." Religion even at its meekest, on the contrary, has to admit no such thing. The religion that moderates participate in has no interest in total solutions of any kind and indeed severely doubts that any such solution is possible or desirable. That what Hitchens has really been discussing is fundamentalism and not religion comes out toward the end of his essay, when he admits that "totalitarian systems, whatever outward form they take, are fundamentalist and, as we would now say, 'faith-based.'"

Wherever we read "religion" in Hitchens's book, then, from the title down to the cascade of catastrophes committed in God's name, we are really meant to read "fundamentalism." Only this can explain how he and other atheists attempt to account for secular political atrocities and why they feel compelled to do so in the first place.

Sam Harris makes a similar move in his book *The End of Faith*. While marketed as an atheist pamphlet (although he does not embrace the moniker and indeed has urged other nonbelievers to avoid adopting any such name for their position) and while making general claims about the evils of religion, the book quickly changes the subject when it tries to account for the crimes of atheism. When faced with what he calls "one of the most common criticisms I encounter," and "also one of the most depressing," namely, that atheist despots were responsible for the worst crimes of the twentieth century, Harris retorts that "while some of the most despicable political movements in human history have been explicitly irreligious, they were not especially rational." But given the way Harris uses the label "rational" in his book, this is about as balanced an assessment as an art critic's deciding that creations from schools of painting he least admires do not qualify as art. Once one has adopted the logic according to which one's own beliefs stand in a one-to-one relation with the world as it really is, one can appeal—as Stalinists certainly did—to reason with the same fervor and with some of the same effects as when religious fundamentalists appeal to God's will. Indeed, almost any prima facie reasonable stance in life can be pushed to an unreasonable extreme. Take the example of Carl Rheinländer, of Koblenz, Germany, who has spent the past decade and a small fortune battling in court for his right not to pay waste-removal fees. Rheinländer's stance is perfectly reasonable. In fact, it is reasonable to the extreme. He has implemented a policy of 100 percent sustainability in his own home. He and his family produce no trash whatsoever. His children wear clothes made of recycled material; all biodegradable materials are composted; all other materials are reused. I have a certain sympathy for Mr. Rheinländer's position, and indeed great admiration for his ambition. Nevertheless, it's readily apparent how perfect rationality with regard to any admirable policy position—be it sustainability, animal rights, or equitable distribution of wealth—would immediately degenerate into a kind of totalitarian nightmare once generalized into a universal obligation. Armed with the kind of certainty provided by the code of codes—which guarantees that your particular passion, plan, or agenda has a direct connection to the totality of reality as it really is in itself—vegetarians can easily become jihadists against backyard barbecuers animal rights activists commit hate crimes against leather-shod pedestrians; and peasants engage in ritual executions of anyone who has been taught how to read. Of course, such extremism does not strike us as rational because we have our own standards for limiting the pursuit of in-themselves rational ends. We understand, implicitly, that even reasonable ends can have reasonable limits placed on them.

"The problem," Harris goes on to admit freely, "is none other than the problem of dogma itself." Naturally, I totally agree. The only way for Harris to pin the history of violence and inhumanity he outlines in his book on the catchall of religion is to ignore those many religious practices and beliefs that are not dogmatic. It is belief in the code of codes, not in the stories of any particular religion, that underlies the sort of certainty about one's own righteousness that is characteristic of religious, ethnic, or nationalist violence.

Can Sam Harris not see the irony? After spending hundreds of pages cataloging and decrying the atrocities committed by religious men who were so certain of their righteousness they would, on the suspicion of the slightest disagreement, submit a fellow human being to the most unimaginable tortures and then burn him alive, he then turns around and defends the use of torture on terror suspects today. The argument he resuscitates is familiar by now: Alan Dershowitz's the-bomb's-about-to-go-off-in-a-major-city scenario, where we find ourselves guilty of complicity in mass homicide if we don't agree to torture the guy we know is guilty anyway. The scenario is tailor-made to make anyone who raises an objection look like the worst sort of emasculated liberal, much like the here's-the-man-who-raped-and-murdered-your-mother scenario did to Michael Dukakis, whose official stance against capital punishment during his 1988 presidential bid made him seem weak and unfeeling in the face of such gut-wrenching evil.

But the answer to both scenarios is, or at least should be, the same. If you were to describe this highly hypothetical situation to me, I would gladly admit that, faced with my mother's tormentor and given the power to do so, I would not only kill him but also cheerfully descend to the worst state of barbarism in doing so. The law, however, has no business helping me out in my revenge. One of the principles of our democracy is that it is, famously, a government of laws, not men. The law is not meant to codify our individual and at times homicidal urgings; it is meant to inscribe an impassive and objective due process ensuring that everyone's rights are protected in an equal way.

Where reality is bumpy and uneven, the law strives not to be. Where reality offers a perfectly endless capacity for nuance and difference in the scenarios that actually crop up on a day-to-day basis, the law describes only a finite series of situations and the requisite responses to those situations. Most important, the ultimate law of the United States, our Constitution and its Bill of Rights, guarantees in far fewer words than any modern equivalent that no person shall be judged without due process of law—which means, for the sake of Sam Harris and ex–attorney general Gonzales, there can be no footnotes for those men we just happen to *know* are terrorists without our having bothered to hold trials to find out. After all, the Church's inquisitors must have been as certain that the women they were torturing were witches as the interrogators in Dershowitz's nightmare scenario are that their subject is the terrorist in question.

Harris's response to this objection is obvious, and quickly countered. I am, like Noam Chomsky and other liberals, simply drawing moral equivalences where none exist, blinded as I must be by the fog of relativism. But the truth is entirely the contrary: I *agree* with Harris that there can be no equivalence between the so-called collateral damage of U.S. bombs and the victims of 9/11. I *agree* that the difference between *trying* to kill as many people as you can and trying *not* to is a valid and valuable one. It is Harris who forgets this distinction when he argues that there is no moral difference between the suffering caused by modern warfare and the suffering we impose on a terror suspect if we torture him, and that we should thus have no qualms about torturing suspects if we are willing to go to war to defend ourselves.

In fact, Harris goes so far as to say that "if there is even one chance in a million that [a terror suspect] will tell us something under torture that will lead to the future dismantling of Al Qaeda, it seems that we should use every means at our disposal to get him talking." Let's take this number seriously for a second. If we assume there are at least three hundred al-Qaeda operatives active in the United States today, then torturing every one of America's three hundred million men, women, and children suddenly seems like a good idea under Harris's logic, because that would pretty much guarantee having a real al-Qaeda operative on our hands and hence of learning something that will lead to al-Qaeda's future dismantling (assuming, that is, that torture is an effective means of securing valuable information, an assumption that has been largely debunked by such real-life interrogators as Matthew Alexander).

The difference between torturing suspects and causing human death and destruction in war is perhaps subtle but, from a legal perspective, very real. That is why we have something called war crimes and an international criminal court to try their perpetrators. For Harris, "if we are willing to drop bombs or even risk that pistol rounds might go astray, we should be willing to torture a certain class of criminal suspects and military prisoners; if we are unwilling to torture, we should be unwilling to wage modern war." My grandfather flew bombing missions over Germany in World War II and, Harris's attempt to draw moral equivalences notwithstanding, he most definitely was not a war criminal. There is nothing "collateral" about the damage a torturer is doing to his victim's body and psyche; every bit of it is as intentional as can be.

What, then, to do about the Dershowitz scenario? Do we just sit by and serve our doomsday bomber another cup of tea while waiting for the mushroom cloud to show up on the horizon? Well, the answer, it seems to me, is quite simple. We need to have the courage of our convictions and pay the logical price for what we believe in. If you are voting for war, then you should be signing up yourself, or at the very least your children should be on the list of the first to be deployed. If you are going to torture a terror suspect, then at the very least you should be willing to spend a long time in prison for doing so. Is that unfair? Not at all. The decision to submit someone to torture cannot and should not be given a cozy legal protection. If we are asking soldiers to die on the battlefield for us every day and subjecting countless others to collateral damage, the least we can tell an interrogator is that he is going to risk his career and livelihood if he makes the decision to turn to illegal means. Perhaps the existence of such clearly stated consequences would lead potential torturers to the conclusion that it makes good sense to interrogate suspects using the time-honored and legal methods outlined in the Army Field Manual on Interrogation.

Lawmakers who have been to war and whose sons and daughters have as well, like Senator Jim Webb of Virginia, are likely to have a more balanced and cautious view of war than the vast majority of legislators, who have neither seen combat nor would ever risk sending a loved one in harm's way. Men like John McCain, who have been in captivity and subjected to torture, are generally unwilling to sanctify the practice as the law of the land. I may be wrong here, but I very much doubt that either Sam Harris or Alan Dershowitz has ever been tortured. Perhaps if they were to sign up for a little waterboarding— as Christopher Hitchens did before concluding unambiguously that if it is not torture then nothing is—it would make their case for the legality of torture more plausible. There is, after all, nothing quite like the golden rule.

At the least, the atheists I have discussed in this chapter are impatient with patience and show little restraint over showing restraint. And why should they? They speak with the same kind of certainty that has enlightened countless religious fanatics in the past. The only difference is that they celebrate the religion of reason, a human faculty deserving of the greatest respect and admiration. Respect and admiration, yes, but not worship. A moderate worships only what he or she can never pretend to understand, and thus will never pretend to speak in its name. When you speak in the very name of reason, as when you speak in the name of God, expect blood to flow. This is why even so reasonable a voice as Hitchens made the mistake of supporting the Bush administration's adventure in Iraq. From his perspective, as from Harris's, "Islamic fascism" is a threat that the West must confront, with force if necessary. Doubtless there are threats in the world that must eventually be confronted with force, although it seemed at the time to many of us what is now almost a consensus: the decision to invade Saddam Hussein's Iraq was an epochal mistake. But there again the devotees of God and the devotees of reason could see eye to eye and waste with their certainty a veritable river of U.S. and Iraqi blood along with much of the livelihood of generations to come.

2 The Fundamentalism of Everyday Life

A Winning Streak

I am not a gambler. The few times I've visited casinos I've usually nursed twenty dollars until it vanished while sipping on a couple of free cocktails. Winning, in other words, has never been a goal, much less a reality.

That all changed one night a couple of winters ago. My family and I were on vacation in Saint-Moritz with my brother-in-law and his family. One evening we decided to take a break from the kids and head over to the casino. As I made the rounds with my drink, my brother-in-law (who, unlike me, really knows his way around a casino) popped up in front of me and excitedly ordered me to tell him a number. I mumbled some excuse about not really believing in such stuff and finally, when he insisted, said the first number that came to my mind.

What transpired that night seemed, at least at the time, remarkable. Between the two of us we hit the right number in roulette eight times. The odds of hitting the right number once in roulette are one in thirty-six. The odds of hitting it twice in a row are one in thirty-six squared, or 1,296. By the end of the evening, when we decided not to push our luck any further, we both felt as though something almost magical had happened. Each time the roulette wheel landed on a number we had bet, it seemed as if we—possessed if only temporarily by some wisdom or vision that others in the room lacked—had known or felt what the number was going to be before the wheel was spun.

Obviously we were wrong. Moreover, we were wrong not merely in thinking that we somehow *knew* or *felt* what the number would be; we were wrong in even thinking that *any given* number *was going to be* the number that came up. In other words, the very grammar of how we understood the situation was wrong.

At the time of the rolling of the wheel, or when the dealer calls for last bets, is it really the case that a *given* number *is going to be* the one the marble lands on? The inventory of forces determining the motion of a marble rolling around a roulette wheel is so extraordinarily complex that not only is it impossible to predict the outcome but *there is in fact no stable outcome* until just before the ball settles. And yet when we think of betting on an outcome, we often think in terms of an outcome that was *going to happen* and that we chanced upon through luck or special insight.

In going back over the events of that night, I quickly saw that overall I had a lot less to marvel at than originally seemed to be the case. One person placing single bets on single numbers, always placing the winnings from one bet on the next number and having each of them come in eight times in a row, would not only constitute an unprecedented event in the history of gambling but also break the house in any casino in the world. (According to my shirt-cuff calculations, a one dollar bet under such circumstances would pay out almost three trillion dollars, an amount only the U.S. government could bankroll, and with rather undesirable consequences for the economy!) This was, unfortunately, not what happened that evening.

While we now remember only the eight times we won, at the time my brother-in-law and I were planted at the roulette table for something close to three hours. Furthermore, we hedged our bets, placing so-called split, street, or square bets, in which the chips are placed on two, three, or four numbers respectively. We were up by the end of the evening, yes, but only by 600 francs or so (and about as many free drinks), which suggests that we placed an awful lot of bets that evening in order for those eight wins to pay off.

Finally, we were two out of a good two hundred gamblers at the casino that evening. While our luck seemed extraordinary and wonderful to us, it was certainly not out of the ordinary that someone would be lucky that evening, given that quite a few others would be going home with lightened pockets. If you win the lottery, it may seem like God is smiling on you, but for everyone else who played, it might as well be any other losing day.

Okay, so I was a bit superstitious that night. If I don't tend to be so in general, I can still be forgiven, under the circumstances. What, in the end, is the big deal about thinking, without even being aware of it at the time, that a *given* number was going to be selected as opposed to *some* number being selected? As it turns out, a lot.

In thinking that an outcome somehow preexisted the spinning of the roulette wheel, I was participating in a pervasive and ultimately false way of thinking about the world. This worldview depends on several basic assumptions. First, that things and events exist on a stable time line stretching from the past into the future that we living beings experience one moment at a time. According to this view, it actually makes a lot of sense to assume that in the moment a roulette wheel is spun there is going to be a given outcome, one that we just don't know yet. In fact, according to this view there is a given outcome awaiting every spinning of every roulette wheel from now until the end of time. If we don't know the outcomes, that's just because our ability to know is limited by time. We simply don't see the future the same way we see the present and saw the past.

The second assumption underlying this worldview is that the universe as it stretches out in space and time is ultimately *knowable as it really is in itself*. As this may not be entirely clear, let me explain. Philosophers since Plato have pointed out that there may indeed be a difference between how we perceive the world and how it really is. As we know from the science of optics, for example, the greenness of trees is an attribute of how the frequency of light waves reflected off the leaves' surfaces interacts with the human retina. The leaves are therefore green only *for us*, not *in themselves*.

For the world to be knowable in itself, it would have to be so in such a way that whoever is doing the knowing is not limited by such pesky circumstances as retinas and light waves or position in space and time. But the only being who could know something—and not just something, everything, the universe as a whole—without such limitations as having a body or using a medium like light would be an omniscient being along the lines of what monotheistic traditions call God. Therefore, the two assumptions I've just outlined—that the world consists of things and events that exist on a stable time line stretching from the past into the future and that those things and events are ultimately knowable as they are in themselves—entail a fundamentally religious way of seeing the world . . . make that a *fundamentalist* way of seeing the world. For while it can be religious, fundamentalism can manifest itself in just about any way you can imagine. In this chapter the aim is to grasp what this kind of fundamentalist thinking is all about and how it affects our everyday lives.

The Logic of Codes

The great Argentine writer Jorge Luis Borges once imagined what the universe would be like if it were to take the form of a library. This library, he wrote, would consist of interlocking hexagons, the walls of each containing a certain number of bookshelves and books, each containing a certain number of pages and lines. The inhabitants of the library would wander the hexagons for years, decades, and generations, trying to discover the meaning of their existence in the pages of these books. While no single book in the library is identical to any other, Borges writes, what is certainly the case is that every possible combination of the letters of the alphabet is to be found in its volumes. Among volumes and volumes of nonsense, in other words, there exist the complete works of Shakespeare, as well as another version of the same that's missing one letter, another missing two, and so on.

The remarkable insight of Borges's tale lies in how the narrator, himself lost in this universe of signs, describes the inevitability of religion. By a seemingly flawless deduction, the library's scholars theorize the existence of a book of books, a book that contains a perfect explanation of the otherwise unorganized and overwhelming morass of information. Since every book exists, they reason, this one too must exist, and in its pages someone has read or at some point will read the ultimate meaning and purpose of the library, and that person has become or will become enlightened. The narrator himself is uncertain about this hypothesis, but he expresses a hope that someday, someone, even if he himself will never know of it, will discover the ultimate meaning of the library, and that in this discovery the library itself and the existence of so many searchers will be justified.

I recount this story because it poses the problem of religious belief in terms of *codes*. A code is a set of instructions for producing something. All that is required for it to be a code is that if a competent person, machine, or process follows the instructions faithfully, it will in fact produce the function or body to which the code corresponds. For instance, a secret code, such as the famous Enigma code used by the Germans in World War II, is a set of instructions for producing a message. When received by a person competent in decoding it, the message can be faithfully reproduced. The code used by the software I am writing with at this moment is a set of instructions that, when decoded by my computer or one belonging to another potential reader, will result in the reproduction of the text I am writing. Finally, the genetic code carried in our DNA provides the instructions for combining amino acids in such a way as to build the proteins that make up our bodies.

It is precisely because of the enormous strides made in the fields of computing and genetics that the idea of code has taken on such importance in the past half century, as I'll show in the next chapter. But for the time being what is essential to note is that at the heart of the different kinds of code—communicative, technological, biological—a similar function is involved. Not only messages but also the images we interact with and the very living tissue we are made of can be mined for their hidden codes.

What we can learn from Borges's story is that once we identify *encoding* as a basic function in the world—once we see the world as something like a giant library of symbols combining and recombining in ways that make up the visible world—there may be a natural tendency to think of this very encoding function as itself hiding a code. This *code of codes* would be, then, something akin to the "language of God" with which the molecular biologist Francis Collins labeled the fully sequenced human genome, but on a far vaster scale.

Religion and science are two human endeavors that set out to explore the world and seek the truth and are thus two domains in which the logic of the code of codes can best be seen at work. We don't have to do much digging, however, to find this logic at work in politics and culture as well. In this chapter you'll see how the religious logic of the code of codes influences how we vote, how laws are made, who is included in certain institutions and who excluded, what causes we give our money to, and in some cases who will live and who will die.

The Truth Is Out There

There's a scene in the movie *A Beautiful Mind* in which the schizophrenic and eventual Nobel laureate John Forbes Nash stands before a wall of news clippings and begins to detect patterns that no one else can see. As the camera pans the wall we see individual articles and sentences emerge from an undifferentiated background and start to connect with one another in a complex latticework of hidden meaning. While it is eventually revealed that what seemed to be a special insight was in fact a symptom of Nash's mental illness, the scene is symptomatic of a general and widespread belief that daily life holds secrets that are hidden from the uninitiated and that people with special talents or vision can unlock.

While there is nothing new about the idea of secret codes and of the special knowledge needed to break them, it does seem that we are living in a time that has been witness to a particular proliferation of the code motif. New Age self-help books and movies like *The Secret*, which claims to reveal the hidden key to success and happiness in everyday life, have achieved super–best seller status; Giorgio Armani released a perfume called Code; and in the summer of 2003, a relatively little-known writer and former schoolteacher from New Hampshire published what would soon become one of the best selling books of all time. *The Da Vinci Code* has gone to spawn two major films (the second based on an earlier Dan Brown novel, *Angels and Demons*) as well as inspire the curiosity of those who never knew they were conspiracy buffs, the disdain of serious historians dismayed that his fictions are taken by so many to be fact, and the wrath of religious

defenders for whom Dan Brown's novels are nothing short of a rela-
tivistic attack on the foundations of faith.

In fact, *The Da Vinci Code* is a potboiler of a thriller, a quick summer read about a Harvard "symbologist" who has to run from the
French police when they tag him for the murder of a famous curator
at the Louvre Museum. On the run across Europe with a (naturally)
beautiful young "cryptologist" from the Paris police department, Robert Langdon must decipher a series of codes, beginning with the mys-
teriously arranged murder scene at the Louvre, that lead him deeper
and deeper into a two-thousand-year-old plot by the Roman Catholic
hierarchy to hide secrets about the human nature of Jesus Christ.

That a book whose central story involves the secret sexual and family life of Jesus would go on to sell in excess of 40 million copies certainly irked many Christians, and not a few articles and books were
published that pointed to *The Da Vinci Code*'s many historical errors
and lambasted Brown as a heretic. Some of the authors of these criticisms also paused to wonder why his book had sold so many copies,
thus putting the faith of so many believers in danger. Kenneth Boa
and John Alan Turner, for instance, argued that post-9/11 America had
lost its way and was in search of answers to ground a kind of existen-
tial malaise, and that while some of those answers came in the form
of an increased interest in spirituality, as evidenced by the crowds that
flocked to buy Rick Warren's *The Purpose-Driven Life* or to see Mel Gib-
son's *The Passion of the Christ*, the same feelings of being unanchored
led readers to the false certainties revealed by *The Da Vinci Code*.

Boa and Turner are convinced that the cause for this lamentable
embrace of a heretic writer is the "postmodern world" we live in. They
cite approvingly an article in the *Family Therapy Networker* from 1991
that describes said world as being shaped by "pluralism, democracy,
religious freedom, consumerism, mobility and increasing access to
news and entertainment." The article goes on to lament that "residents
of this postmodern world are able to see that there are many beliefs,
multiple realities, and an exhilarating but daunting proliferation of
world views—a society that has lost its faith in absolute truth and in
which people have to choose what to believe." Adrift in relativism
and cynicism, Americans were caught by 9/11 without the protections
offered by certainty and deeply held religious faith. As Boa and Turner

conclude, "people who left their faith behind realized that when catastrophe happens, the desire to cling to a transcendent God resurfaces."

There may well be something to this analysis, at least as far as the apparent resurgence of interest in spirituality in the early years of this millennium is concerned. But what Dan Brown's critics misunderstand is that, far from being a representative of "pluralism, democracy, religious freedom" and every other tendency anathema to their orthodox faiths, Brown's novel evinces exactly the same, fundamentalist structure that their own beliefs do. Hard-pressed to differentiate the appeal of *The Da Vinci Code* from that of other cultural blockbusters of the same period, the authors fail to realize that there is a very good, very simple reason for this: when frightened by catastrophe we reach for certainty, and there is something very reassuring about the idea that underneath the complexity and apparent contradictions of everyday life a simple truth lies hidden. Fundamentalism is comforting. It tells us that confusion, complexity, and contradiction are illusions masking a simple reality, and that to reach that reality we need only break the code. When 40 million readers spent a summer enjoying Dan Brown's thriller, they were motivated by the same conviction that underlies the power of all fundamentalisms: the truth is out there, you just need to find it.

It probably makes sense at this point to make something perfectly clear. By criticizing the belief that "the truth is out there" I am not thereby criticizing truth or embracing so-called postmodern relativism (although I confess a certain fondness for democracy and pluralism). Rather, what I am questioning is the belief that the truth in question is *out* there, that is, that it already exists as a kind of knowledge, waiting to be discovered, copied down, or translated. Truths, in other words, are statements about the world; they are not things we can round up and measure but statements about the things we round up and measure. That means that we can compare statements as regards their truth value, criticize them, and ultimately reject some as false without ever accepting the idea that the truth itself is out there prior to our formulating it.

Dan Brown's extraordinary success with *The Da Vinci Code* is only the most obvious example of the logic of the code of codes, which has been used to great success in fiction, film, television, and the self-help industry. Millenarian fiction such as the popular *Left Behind* series capitalizes on this literal version of the code of codes, as do television series such as *Lost* and *Heroes*. But popular fiction and television don't just provide examples of how the code of codes entices our interest, they are part of a cultural landscape that primes us to think and act in certain ways in many other aspects of our lives.

The Truth Is in Here?

If truth is not out there, it's just as much an illusion to think it's in us, waiting to be discovered. "This above all: to thy own self be true" ranks among the greatest platitudes that Shakespeare ever put into any character's mouth, and yet for the modern individual in the postindustrial West such platitudes apparently constitute the deepest philosophical insights. Multimillion-dollar industries are dedicated to pursuing the "return" to one's true self, a self lost in the world of products, choices, and workaday doldrums those very industries grind out day by day. From over-the-counter cosmetics to cosmetic surgery, for example, the discourse of self-help and self-improvement is explicitly expressed in terms of recapturing or rediscovering one's true self; makeover is required only insofar as the true self has gone out of focus, has lost its original luster.

The fundamental presupposition of the fundamentalism of everyday life, then, is that the self in its truth is naked, pure, unadorned. Only insofar as the self degenerates—over time, through distraction, stress, lack of attention—does it need the help of some cosmetic alteration to return to its original state. But what this fundamentalist illusion hides is the fact that there is no pure, naked self but always a self-in-alteration, a self constructing itself out of countless layers of adornment, display, acting, both for itself and for the gaze and expectations of others.

In the context of his insightful study of Americans' obsession with what have come to be known as enhancement technologies, Carl Elliott quotes a line from Almodóvar's movie *All About My Mother*, in which the transsexual Agrado says, "A woman is more authentic the more she looks like what she has dreamed for herself." It is a marvelous line, not least because it is spoken by a male-to-female transsexual who, at that moment in the film, has taken the stage to announce the cancellation of a performance of *A Streetcar Named Desire* and has offered to entertain those who wish to stay with the story of her life. The monologue she performs for an increasingly appreciative audience is all about the effort, the performance, in fact, required to become authentic, to become what Carl Elliott refers to as one's true self. Elliott's point in quoting the line is, correctly I believe, to defend the notion that an authentic self can indeed be something quite other than what one has been born as, or trained by one's culture to believe one actually is. Drawing on the work of Lionel Trilling and others, Elliott describes a history of authenticity in which the idea of what one is in one's most intimate core has changed from a series of characteristics that were viewed as in some sense unchanging, and were known as "character," to a more pliable, fungible ideal, namely "personality."

Unlike a person's character, which is principally a moral entity, personality, which began to emerge in self-help literature in the early twentieth century, is something that can be cultivated. To the extent that the index of the true self changes from a given character to a constructed or performed personality, Elliott argues, it becomes natural for technologies that at another time might be seen as secondary or accidental to authenticity—technologies dedicated to enhancing the self rather than, say, restoring what was already there—to become accepted aspects of finding or achieving the true self.

The way was thus well prepared for reality makeover shows like ABC's *Extreme Makeover* and Fox's *The Swan* when they appeared in the early years of the twenty-first century. The crescendo of reality television over the past decade has coincided with a mounting interest in the abilities of plastic surgery to remake the face and body. The result in the case of *The Swan*: a real-life beauty pageant whose contestants, rather than hide their recourse to surgical technology, proudly and publicly reveal it. In the words of *The Swan*'s producers, we tune in to behold "the amazing transformation" these contestants undergo. The pageant is unique, they say, because unlike any other it takes into account not only beauty and poise but also "overall transformation." And, indeed, the transformations are astounding. Unlike with traditional beauty pageants, we are captivated not only by the beauty on display but also, and perhaps far more intensely, by the ugliness from which the beauty has been wrought. Different from other pageants, then, *The Swan* is also an ugliness contest. If the women look more or less the same at the end, the real specificity of the amazing transformation lies in how they looked before they began.

The Swan plays out a fantasy before our eyes, a fantasy born of the miscegenation of consumerism with the modern obsession with self-realization. This fantasy, which we could call the desire for limitless change, promises that the drive to self-realization can be fulfilled through consumerism, through choosing and applying various products, solutions, or changes and expressing them directly on the body. This fantasy is a continuation and elaboration of that tendency in American culture, noted by critics of modern culture from Marx to Weber to Heidegger, toward an ever-increasing instrumentalization of all aspects of life, to the point where the human body, previously considered the necessary presupposition of all experience, becomes yet another in an apparently endless series of tools to be implemented in the quest for individual fulfillment. In the Marxian vision, of course, the body is ultimately deployed in the service of capital, such that *The Swan*'s message to viewers could best be paraphrased along the lines of a commercial for the next "miracle" hair conditioner, "Why shouldn't I buy it? I'm worth it." Only this time, what is being bought is not merely something to apply to the body but in fact a new body.

What is crucial to recognize, however, is that the fantasy of limitless change that is played out before our eyes, a fantasy that exists to support capitalism's fantasy of infinite choice, is itself nothing but an illusion. It is not, however, an illusion for the simple reasons one might expect: that the body has limitations, that you can change it only so far, and so on. In fact it is true the surgeon's blades and lasers can perform astonishing transformations. What is unlimited by technology, however, is finally limited by the models and templates society provides; as has been widely commented, beauty as fashioned by technology is all too familiar. Rather than technology's limitless capacity for transformation being a catalyst for divergence, it becomes one for convergence; from a diverse wealth of ugliness comes a monolithic poverty of beauty.

Over and over again we hear the same justification for pursuing physical transformation: the change enables the contestant to find his or her *own true self*. As Brenda Weber has written, quoting a contestant from ABC's *Extreme Makeover*, "I'm me now," an exclamation that seems to capture the general sentiment of the makeover ideology: change oneself in order to better become oneself. It would be hard to find examples of makeover TV where this mantra is not at the very least implied. The reasons for this are in part legal. As Bernadette Wegenstein has investigated in her documentary film *Made Over in America*, contestants on *The Swan* are screened for possible cases of body dysmorphic disorder (BDD), a condition defined as "a preoccupation with an imagined or slight defect in appearance." Common questions intended for identifying this disorder concern how often, for example, an individual imagines him- or herself with a different nose. By attempting to exclude sufferers of BDD, and thus focusing the rhetoric of selection on a healthy relationship to self-identity, the show's producers intend to ward off the potential criticism that they are essentially helping sick individuals get sicker. Yet the irony is that *no articulation of a desire for self-modification can be rigorously excluded as abnormal or aberrant vis-à-vis a normal desire*, because the desire for self-modification is by its very nature simultaneously rooted in a self as it is perceived to be and directed at a vision of self as it could be but is not. Insofar as all bodies are changing, and as all subjects participate in that change in a desiring and embodied way, we are all examples of BDD: our bodies are dysmorphic in that they refuse to remain in a given shape over time; and they are equally disordered in that our desires always perceive them as dislocated from a common order, the order of perfect attractiveness or desirability.

Now, my point in making this argument is not to ridicule or otherwise undermine what may be a perfectly useful diagnostic category; I am sure there are people who truly suffer something along the lines of what is described by BDD in a clinically urgent way. My point, rather, is to question the logic of exclusion by which shows such as *The Swan* try to guarantee that what is at stake in their modification projects is the attainment of a permanent, ideal self underlying all the changes we go through. By excluding, impossibly, those cases in which the model of change to be pursued is aberrant or alien, the show implicitly claims that the goal is natural, an extension of the contestant's identity. At the same time, however, the rhetoric of the producers never ceases to highlight the radical nature of the transformation, a transformation that is more than "skin deep" because, of course, it allows the beauty that was always there on the inside to emerge to the surface.

The Trouble with Nuance

It has often been said that the United States at the turn of the twenty-first century is in the midst of a culture war. Although one may certainly argue with the bellicose terminology, as well as with the specificity of the claim to this time and place, the focus on culture is quite apt. The political divisions registered in the 2000, 2004, and 2008 presidential elections often seemed less about specific policy differences between two parties that are, for the most part, entrenched and beholden to elites to relatively the same degree than about what kind of culture each party claims as its constituency. For all the necessary debunking the notion of red and blue states has undergone, for instance, the geographical association of "America's heartland," or what Sarah Palin has called the real America, with a certain kind of culture and the costal and northern urban centers with another continues to hold the popular imagination. The heartland culture is, as its vociferous champions proudly proclaim, conservative. Its constituents uphold "traditional" values like family, religion, and nation and disdain the people they call liberals for betraying these core values. The so-called liberal culture is supposed to be, in contrast, progressive, inclusive and tolerant of otherness, and dedicated to social equality.

If one pays attention to the basic structure of the rhetoric, however, one can discern an undercurrent, and perhaps a more fundamental basis of conflict. Conservative culture is captivated by the idea of simplicity. Underneath the multiplicity of appearances, conservatives believe, are a few very simple truths: freedom is preferable to tyranny; the traditional family is the foundation of a functional society; there is good and there is evil and very little in between. It can be no surprise that a film like *Forrest Gump*, about how a simple but good man triumphs over adversity and complicated political interests, had such powerful appeal in Middle America. Those whose basic belief system is built on such presuppositions look with suspicion on those who believe the world to be inherently complex. They think that people who constantly point to complexity are muddying up the issues, failing to look at the big picture. Worse, they may be purposely obfuscating in order to pursue their own narrow interests. Liberals, for their part, really do tend to believe that the world is more complicated than conservatives imply and decry the tendency on the right to view reality in such starkly simplified terms.

This rhetoric has dominated political life in the United States over the past decades as the right has used it to greater and greater political effect. The Republican Party's success in casting John Kerry as a "flip-flopper," for instance, more interested in "nuance" and other French-sounding values than in core issues of right and wrong, was a key factor in the 2004 presidential race. But the crucial point to recognize is that the binary of simplicity versus complexity extends to all areas of the current cultural conflict. The academic "theater" of the culture war, for example, pits those who feel that the basic drive of the human and natural sciences is the pursuit of a single, unified truth against those who ostensibly waste their time obscuring that truth with pointless distinctions and deviating from it in the service of narrow political interests. The so-called postmodern tendency in the humanities has been endlessly criticized for this perceived failing in blatantly right-wing books like *Tenured Radicals*, *The Closing of the American Mind*, and *Illiberal Education* as well as in attacks by self-proclaimed leftists, such as Sokal and Bricmont's *Fashionable Nonsense*. It was in this spirit that Jonathan Kandell's roundly criticized obituary in the *New York Times* for Jacques Derrida in October 2004 refused to mention him as a philosopher, referring to him instead as an "abstruse theorist."

The political team around the second President Bush often made little secret of their use of this strategy. It is clear that the potential voters and taxpayers who lent their support to "the war on terror" and the war in Iraq in the early years of the twenty-first century did so largely and often because of their belief in a certain reality projected beyond the appearances. The Bush representation apparatus, for example, was successful in convincing vast swaths of voters that behind the necessary and lamentable apparatus of representation—the polls, the concocted photo ops, the faked newscasts and staged "town hall" meetings— President Bush was a man of "character." Indeed, as was widely reported and fretted about, many Americans cited issues of character and value as the reason they voted for him in 2004. The paradox is that no one is (or very few are) actually taken in by the performance, in the sense of not realizing that it is a performance; the fundamentalist influence is exerted when, in the very midst of the performance and in full knowledge of its artifice, the viewer becomes convinced that the artifice in fact refers to some truth just beyond the camera's glare.

This effect is not limited to outright political representation, such as the campaign programming or the manipulation of the news media that was so prevalent during the lead-up to the Iraq War. The entertainment industry in general can be counted on to produce contents for television and film that cohere with the overall message coming from the centers of political power. As the philosopher Slavoj Žižek wrote in an article in the *Guardian*, for instance, the wildly successful Fox series *24*, in which Kiefer Sutherland plays a government antiterrorism agent, abetted in certain, very specific ways the administration's efforts to minimize criticism of its handling of terror suspects. The show's hook is that it plays in "real" time and that each of the season's twenty-four-hour-long episodes corresponds to an hour of one continuous day in the life of agent Jack Bauer. While the show is obviously fiction, and no one among its producers or probably anyone watching it would argue the opposite, precisely in its function as artifice it refers implicitly to a reality that is "out there," beyond representation, independent of its fictitious message. Because everyone can comfortably agree that this is the case, we the viewers end up being force-fed a "neutral" and "independent" reality that is in fact a very specific political version of reality. In the case of *24*, the "real time" of the narrative (which, as Žižek points out, is augmented by the fact that even the time for commercial breaks is counted among the sixty minutes) contributes to the sense of urgency that, for example, if Jack and his well-meaning colleagues don't get the answers they need, by whatever means necessary, millions of innocent people will die in a catastrophic terrorist event. In such circumstances we obviously have to have some flexibility around issues like the torture of detainees.

Thus the success of the code of codes lies in how it convinces us that behind every complex reality lies a simpler—and thus more attractive—truth. When 24's Jack Bauer tortures yet another terror suspect, his methods seem justified by the enormity of the threat. Shades of gray are a luxury for peaceful times, the show seems to be telling us; when the stakes are high we need someone who will reveal the truth by whatever means possible.

Beyond its pervasiveness in our cultural milieu, the fundamentalism of everyday life produced by our belief in the code of codes has affected even how we decide guilt and innocence in the context of the war on terror. In 2005 a young Pakistani-American named Hamid Hayat was arrested on charges of providing material support to terrorists, a charge for which he was convicted in 2006. At the trial, the challenge for federal prosecutors was to prove his intent. In addition to his videotaped confession, which was all but inadmissible given the way he "repeatedly contradicted himself" and "parroted the answers that agents suggested," as Amy Waldman documented in her excellent coverage of this case for the *Atlantic*, the only piece of evidence was a folded scrap of paper that had been found in his wallet with a phrase written in Arabic. Consequently, as in many recent anti-terrorism cases, the arguments ended up revolving around a battle of opposing interpretations. As Judge Gerald Rosen remarked in the context of another recent case, "I think the jury will be overjoyed to hear another expert on Islamic fundamentalism," and his irony was not misplaced. Indeed, many of such cases have come down to little more than battling assertions between scholars of Islam and Arabic who themselves have strong ideological positions on current geopolitics and can earn some $250 an hour for their testimony to boot.

Curiously, the translated Arabic phrase was not so controversial. It reads something along the lines of "Oh Allah, we place you at their throats and seek refuge in you from their evil." What was a source of controversy was whether the act of carrying such a phrase around on a piece of paper signified something specific about the character and intent of the person in question. The prosecution turned to Khaleel Mohammed, an assistant professor of religious studies at San Diego State University, who testified that "just about every commentary I checked puts [the supplication] in a case where someone who is in jihad makes this supplication, someone who is at war with a perceived enemy."

Hayat was convicted on four counts, but many Pakistanis Waldman interviewed recognized the practice of carrying a piece of paper with a supplication around on one's person, what is known as a *tawiz*. Furthermore, many even recognized the text in question and called it quite common. As Waldman comments, none of this may prove that Hayat was not a terrorist, but "the prayer's commonness means that it didn't prove that he was." To suggest an analogy, it is as if a Christian or a Jew were to be convicted of a crime on the basis of a snippet they carried around from the Old Testament, which, as we know, has its own share of belligerent language.

Should it be possible to be convicted not for a crime you did commit but for one you might have intended to commit? The very idea seems to beg the question of jurisprudence, for what prudence does the law owe other than to its own limits, to its jurisdiction, to that of which the law can speak. Certainly juries are asked to hand down verdicts concerning intent all the time; the distinction between homicide and manslaughter depends on the notion of premeditation. But to attempt to judge a person's intent in the absence of an actual crime is to erase the boundaries between fact and fantasy, for who does not, perhaps even on a daily basis, contemplate actions he or she would never undertake in real life? When the federal jury in Sacramento convicted Hayat largely on the basis of the piece of scripture he carried in his wallet, they turned into legal precedent a precarious act of reading. No longer subject to interpretation, possessing a quotation from the Koran on a folded and worn piece of paper was now taken to be an indelible cipher on a man's soul, and the scholars hired to translate that cipher were not merely rendering another language into English; they were charged with reading an ultimate and unchangeable knowledge, something akin to the language of God.

The Dangers of Higher Law

In May 2007 the International Association of Athletics Federations (IAAF), the body governing worldwide competition in track and field, initiated proceedings to bar South African runner Oscar Pistorius from competing in the 2008 Olympic Games. Pistorius's times were not up there with the best in the world. His most recent wins at the time matched the best women's times from the 2004 games, and it was in no way certain that he could improve enough to qualify for the Beijing games. So why the preemptive attempt to exclude him? What did Pistorius do to inspire this kind of opprobrium?

What he did, it turns out, was to be born without legs. Oscar Pistorius was born without fibulas and had his legs amputated at the knee while he was still an infant. He runs using a pair of carbon-fiber prostheses called Cheetahs, with which he has managed to achieve some of the extraordinary times just mentioned.

The worry, as far as the IAAF was concerned, was that Pistorius's high-tech appendages offered him an unfair advantage. IAAF director of development Elio Locatelli was quoted by the *New York Times* as saying, "With all due respect, we cannot accept something that provides advantages. It affects the purity of sport. Next will be another device where people can fly with something on their back." In the end, the IAAF did rule him ineligible for the games. Although the IAAF decision was ultimately overturned by the Court of Arbitration for Sport, Pistorius's times did not qualify him for the 2008 Summer Olympics.

When you first look at Pistorius's Cheetahs, the IAAF seems to have a point. Where the human leg is joined by the ankle to the foot, the Cheetahs curve into an elegant and longer blade, reminiscent of the hind legs of those speedy cats for whom the prosthetic limbs were named. Doesn't powerful, resilient carbon fiber sound much stronger and more stable than a mere human tendon?

Nevertheless, the science would seem to suggest otherwise. Lacking a calf muscle or equivalent mechanical replacement, the Cheetahs' carbon-fiber blades return 80 percent of the energy they absorb when they strike the track. This pales in comparison with the rate for an able-bodied runner, whose intact legs can generate up to 240 percent of the energy absorbed when the heel strikes the track. This means that Pistorius's state-of-the-art appendages nonetheless presented him with a serious disadvantage to overcome when racing against the world's top athletes.

But if that's the case, then why did they ignite such resistance on the part of track and field officials? Professor Robert Gailey of the University of Miami Medical School, who researches runners and who came up with the comparative analysis above, thinks he knows why. As he said to Jeré Longman of the *New York Times*, "Are they looking at not having an unfair advantage? Or are they discriminating because of the purity of the Olympics, because they don't want to see a disabled man line up against an able-bodied man for fear that if the person who doesn't have the perfect body wins, what does that say about the image of man?"

It's important to stress that if IAAF officials like Elio Locatelli are indeed harboring the kind of prejudice Gailey describes, it need not be the case that they are aware of it. While Locatelli speaks of the "purity of sport," what he is consciously expressing suspicion of is the technology in Pistorius's Cheetahs. Still, Professor Gailey is asking exactly the right questions. What determines the purity of sport for IAAF officials if not, as Gailey supposes, some kind of preestablished image they have of what the human body really is, in itself, behind the real-life and at times faulty examples of human bodies as they are actually found in the world? This "image of man," in other words, is the international sporting world's version of the code of codes.

The code of codes is also at work in how we make flash judgments about other people on the basis of their gender, race, or ethnicity. On May 21, 2007, Leana Matia was walking with a group of friends from Bushwick Community High School in Brooklyn. Although school was officially in session, the students had been given permission to attend the wake of a friend who had recently been murdered. On the way to the service, they were surrounded by police, who, according to some accounts, pushed some of the students around, cursed at them, and then cuffed them and brought them to the precinct, where they spent the night in holding cells. After having searched them and determined that no one was carrying illegal drugs or concealed weapons, the officers, under the command of Captain Scott Henderson, charged them with unlawful assembly.

For African Americans like Leana and her friends, occurrences like this are, sadly, far from rare. Bob Herbert, who discussed this case in his column in the *Times*, describes her case as exemplifying the harassment minorities suffer at the hands of police in U.S. cities every day. But for Captain Henderson, the arrests were simply part of a plan to deal with troublemakers the police expected to show up at the wake given their suspicion that the murder had been gang related.

It is in light of such questions that racial profiling, the practice of putting certain individuals or groups under special scrutiny because of their race, ethnicity, or religion, has come increasingly under fire. A 2007 report by the Department of Justice found that blacks and Hispanics were three times as likely as whites to be pulled over while driving, and that blacks were twice as likely to be arrested and four times as likely to be subjected to violence. Ironically, earlier studies revealed that although blacks were also twice as likely to be searched for contraband during traffic stops, they were *less likely* than whites to be found carrying any on them.

Reports like this put the lie to claims, like that of Dinesh D'Souza, that racism is a thing of the past. This somewhat startling conclusion in his book *The End of Racism* is based on the distinction he makes between real racism and institutional racism. For D'Souza, real racism is the intentional and consciously experienced perception of someone else as inferior because of his or her race. Institutional racism, in contrast, is visible only statistically, for example, in the documented underperformance of racial minorities. But such statistical evidence, D'Souza insists, does not point to real, intentional racism, which he claims has been all but stamped out since the civil rights movement. Rather, if certain groups fail to excel on standardized tests, it is simply because the individuals so grouped are not working hard enough or are otherwise less capable. Institutional racism, in other words, doesn't exist. It's merely an excuse liberals make for the fact that some groups perform differently from others.

According to this argument, of course, racial profiling wouldn't be a crime; it would be a rationally justifiable aspect of good police work. If certain groups have been shown to engage in a higher incidence of criminal activity, it makes good sense to subject members of that group to a higher level of scrutiny. Critics on the right such as Ann Coulter have been outspoken in their ridicule of our resistance to racial and ethnic profiling in the war on terror, given the overwhelming evidence that members of a specific ethnic and religious group *have* been trying to hurt Americans and *have* been disproportionately responsible for actual acts of terror.

The problem, however, is that D'Souza's distinction between conscious and institutional racism gets everything backward. Institutional or unconscious racism is not only real but also the most pervasive and damaging kind of racism, far more important than the relatively limited cases of bigots acting or speaking in openly bigoted ways. Racial profiling, then, is less of a problem when it is a conscious strategy to match crime-prevention procedures with indexes of group activity than when it results from the unconscious prejudices of law-enforcement officials.

How do we judge? How do we distinguish the illegal practice of harassing minorities on the basis of their race from standard police procedures needed to protect communities from gang violence? Our tendency to think in terms of racial categories has a complex cultural history behind it, but the fact remains that the categories we unconsciously or implicitly use to identify, distinguish, and at times discriminate between groups of people need a *hook* on which to hang. That hook is the code of codes.

In his book *Blink: The Power of Thinking Without Thinking*, Malcolm Gladwell discusses remarkable research that demonstrates the existence of at times extraordinary gaps between the views we consciously attribute to ourselves and the unconscious associations we tend to make between groups of people and certain characteristics. The test he describes is called the Implicit Association Test (IAT), which measures how test subjects associate racial identities or genders with positive or negative ideas. When Gladwell, who is half black, took the test himself, it concluded on the basis of his implicit associations that he had a "moderate preference for whites." (Disclosure: when I took it, it concluded I had a "slight preference for whites.") As Gladwell explains, what the test demonstrates is that

> our attitudes toward things like race or gender operate on two levels. First of all we have our conscious attitudes. That is what we choose to believe. These are our stated values, which we use to direct our behavior deliberately . . . But the IAT measures something else. It measures our second level of attitude, our

racial attitude on an unconscious level—the immediate, *unconscious* associations that tumble out before we've even had time to think.

Such associations are very real and have clear ramifications for society, education, and our legal system. If you are a teacher, are you unthinkingly holding whites to higher standards? If you are a salesman, are you unconsciously hoping for a higher margin when your customers are blacks or women? You may think you would never engage in such behavior, but how would you know it if you did? As Gladwell concludes, what the test shows is that "our unconscious attitudes may be utterly incompatible with our stated conscious values." We can be racists, in other words, and never even know it.

Like the biases revealed by the IAT, belief in the code of codes can often be an unconscious one. That means that we may well have a tendency to believe that our actual perceptions of other people correspond to stable but invisible essences, even if the thought never crosses our conscious minds. To continue with the problem of racial identity, the philosopher K. Anthony Appiah has made the perhaps counterintuitive argument that race literally doesn't exist. What he means is that, although we are quick to categorize a person as being black or white, these designators don't have a one-to-one relation with any concrete characteristics or traits. People exist across a biological spectrum of differently colored skin, and while recent research has begun to locate specific gene sequences for certain racial traits, there is often more overall genetic variance between people living in different parts of Africa than there is between some Africans and some non-African peoples. There is no single gene, in other words, for race.

Yet when we think of a particular group or associate a characteristic with a racial marker, we are implicitly grounding that association on the idea that there is something like a core identity connecting the various individuals displaying that racial marker. According to this logic, individuals are black or white only insofar as there is something real, physical, or biological underlying that definition, an invisible *something* to which the category corresponds.

What if this assumption is simply not true? What if, in other words, as Appiah has argued, there is no essence to being black or white, and instead these labels are attached to groups as they develop historically and culturally and are thus always subject to variation over time? Once we have assumed that people, like the world itself, are defined by essences that underlie how they appear to us, and that those essences can ultimately be read like a piece of code, then we have already subjected the individuals to the violence of an interpretation that is beyond their control. Just ask Leana Matia.

As with the roulette marble that I believed, without even being aware of it and prior to its being spun, was *going to land* on a given number, we may pass judgments on a person's essence without being aware that we are doing so, long before we even meet him or her. But the only reason we can do this is because we believe there's an essence there to be judged in the first place, a code there to be read. If we can train ourselves to think otherwise, if we can realize that neither the world out there nor the genes determining our traits were written so as to correspond with our knowledge of them, to be interpreted in light of our own conceptions or misconceptions of the world, then we will become a lot less arrogant. And one of the unfortunate character traits of modern society that could diminish as a result of this loss of arrogance is our tendency to make snap judgments about others on the basis of the color of their skin.

Not Tying the Knot

The attorney's closing statement was straightforward and powerful: the plaintiffs seeking the protection of the law "lacked both the reasoning and way of life suited to human beings as well as those things which all people habitually accept" as defining marriage. For the state to extend the legal status in question to the plaintiffs would change the very definition of that legal status, effectively destroying it.

If you guessed that this argument was drawn from a recent case about the right of gays to marry, you'd be wrong. These arguments were made by the Spanish theologian Juan de Sepúlveda as he debated the Jesuit Fray Bartolomé de las Casas in 1550 before a court in Seville and concerned not the legal status of marriage—I threw in "marriage" at the end of the quote—but the question of whether

Native Americans should be granted the full legal status of human beings, which would protect them from being enslaved by the Spanish government.

Sepúlveda based his arguments on a notion of "natural slavery," derived from Aristotle and in part from Saint Thomas Aquinas, that suggested that members of communities whose practices were found to be in violation of "natural law" could be deemed less than fully human and hence worthy of enslavement. Although defenders of the traditional definition of marriage as exclusively between a man and a woman are loath to admit it, their arguments are virtually identical to those used in the past to defend the separation and exclusion of certain groups from rights and protections guaranteed to others.

There's a good reason why defenders of traditional marriage resist this association. The presumption of a higher law than human legislation to which we are all naturally subjected invites skepticism and can certainly be interpreted as an unwarranted intrusion of religion into the law. Traditional-marriage proponents are sensitive to such perceptions and complain that, as Margaret Somerville has expressed it, even "good secular reasons to oppose same-sex marriage are re-characterized [by advocates for same-sex marriage] as religious or as based on personal morality and, therefore, as not applicable at a societal level."

Because of this, traditionalists make an effort to couch their arguments against gay marriage in terms emphasizing the practical, social goods that traditional marriage provides. Recognizing that even such a positive litany would not be enough to justify the exclusion of other kinds of marriage, though, they further argue that this traditional definition of marriage and the goods it provides would be destroyed by extending it to include gays.

According to a friend-of-the-court brief submitted by three profamily nongovernmental organizations to the Maryland Court of Appeals as it prepared to hear arguments in a 2006 landmark case, "genderless marriage is a radically different institution than man/woman marriage, as evidenced by the large divergence in the nature of their respective social goods." Moreover, "adoption of genderless marriage will necessarily de-institutionalize man/woman marriage and thereby cause the loss of its unique social goods."

These unique social goods supposedly derive from a particular definition of marriage as being exclusively between and a man and a woman, but the brief provides no argument as to why it is this definition, as opposed to other aspects of the institution, that is responsible for the social goods it is said to produce. In what sense is a particular definition beneficial for society? If a list of benefits is good for society, then they are good for all members of society, gays as well, unless evidence is presented that gays make worse parents, for example, which has never been established.

In fact, the traditional definition of marriage protects nothing that an expanded definition would not also protect, other than the "natural" meaning of marriage that the social institution argument claims not to need. In the words of another friend-of-the-court brief in the Maryland case, "marriage requires a man and a woman in the same way that a hydrogen atom requires an electron and a proton." Marriage, in other words, must be defended in legislation so as not to pervert what it really is in itself, as written in the code of codes.

What exactly is the problem, then, with basing one's defense of traditional marriage on natural law? Why is it so dangerous to believe that our human institutions correspond to another, higher law, written in the code of codes? While the invocation of an underlying, unchanging truth makes arguments from natural law susceptible to being interpreted as nothing more than liturgy in legal dressing, not all of them fall prey to this limitation. After all, some of the founding texts of our republic make declarations that blatantly cite natural and even divine law. "We hold these truths to be self-evident," for example, paves the way for one of the foundational statements for all equal-protection clauses: "all men are created equal."

The more profound problem with arguments based on either a divine or in some other sense higher principle is that one can always subject that principle to misinterpretation. If there is such a thing as natural law, for example, most people would argue today that slavery must violate that law, even though it was held by natural-law proponents in the past to be permissible. Obviously, then, many people have in fact committed gross violations of natural law while supposedly acting in its name, violations that include a terrific variety of exclusions and degradations of other human beings merely because they exhibited some difference in appearance, belief, or practice.

As it happens, a good number of the philosophers associated with the history of natural law were much more tentative about its application than are those who would deploy it today. Aquinas, for example—who defined the goals of marriage as the procreation and education of children and the mutual physical and emotional support of spouses—was more interested in using science to explore the natural law than in proposing legislation on the basis of a law that humans could know only incompletely.

Medieval and Renaissance scientists, keen on learning how to read the "book of nature" to discover its laws, were consistently circumspect about the abilities of human reason to adequately grasp the divine intention behind the world they discovered through science.

As I mentioned in the first chapter, it was Aquinas himself who originally framed the argument for intelligent design, the theory that some aspects of nature are of such inherent complexity that they could not have come about by chance but must have been designed by a creator with a purpose in mind. Yet his purpose was never to replace scientific inquiry with the certainty of creation. Instead, Aquinas was looking for clues in nature about the natural law, clues as to how nature worked. He was asking questions, and the question of God's intention was what led him to further questioning.

In contrast, today's intelligent design movement replaces questions with answers. To the question of how might a trait whose complexity appears irreducible have come about naturally, intelligent design replies simply, "It didn't, it was made that way." Whether arguing for the intelligent design of nature or the natural essence of man-woman marriage, the current adherents of natural law always claim to know the answer before they ask the question. Instead of asking how something complex came about, they answer that it was designed that way. Instead of asking what marriage can be, they answer what they already know marriage to be.

It is perhaps worth considering that past thinkers who believed strongly in the truth of natural law have ultimately tended toward a radical rejection of human attempts to legislate in its name. Lysander Spooner, a nineteenth-century legal theorist, eventually became a convinced anarchist because he feared that any attempt by humans to impose laws would ultimately pervert the real intent of the natural law, thus institutionalizing relations of power between those who were in the position to influence legislation and those who were not. As he wrote, "the real motives and spirit which lie at the foundation of all legislation—notwithstanding all the pretenses and disguises by which they attempt to hide themselves—are the same today as they always have been. The whole purpose of this legislation is simply to keep one class of men in subordination and servitude to another."

If we believe that the law is already written, that it already exists somewhere and that our humble attempts to write legislation are nothing but faint and faulty copies of the code of codes, then perhaps we should, like Spooner, rightfully fear any legislation that excludes one set of humans from an institution, a right, or a social good. If, on the contrary, we believe that laws are pragmatic constructs, made by humans for the sake of dealing with the particular problems of a given time and place, then we must forfeit our claims to defend certain laws because they better represent a divine or natural truth.

In the absence of evidence that extending a privilege to others does damage to society, it is better to err on the side of inclusiveness. For to do the opposite, to insist on exclusion without basis, is to repeat the errors of those who thought they had read the code of codes and were proven wrong.

What About Human Rights?

Despite clashing on many issues during the campaign for the presidency of the United States, Senators Barack Obama and John McCain were essentially of a mind when it came to the use of the U.S. base in Guantánamo Bay, Cuba, as a center for the indefinite detainment of those designated as enemy combatants by the Bush administration. That they both favored closing the facility is not in itself paradoxical; overall there are quite a few issues that political opponents might ultimately agree on. What is most striking is the rationale behind their intent. Billed as the candidate of hope and carried to office on a wave of youth, idealism, and hope for a better world, the United States' first black president famously campaigned on a message of change—changing the present direction of U.S. politics, of course, but also the way politics proceeds in the United States domestically and in U.S. relations with the world. Part of this change involved regaining the nation's stature in international circles and repairing its reputation abroad. Closing Guantánamo and ensuring the cessation of torture and extraordinary rendition would be steps in support of this broader goal. For McCain, a former air force pilot who spent five years as a prisoner of war enduring untold suffering at the hands of his captives, the reason behind closing Guantánamo and ending executive permissiveness around the torture of terror suspects was in some ways far simpler. It responded to a moral imperative: Americans do not and should not condone or practice torture. Thus, while the cold war warrior and arch supporter of the neoconservatives' aggressions in Iraq opposed torture on moral grounds, the new hero of liberals and idealists the world over opposed it on merely pragmatic grounds. The ground had definitely shifted; where idealism was once supposedly the domain of the left, the Obama revolution placed its bets not on ideology or even ideals but on pragmatism, on the philosophy of what works.

The philosophical school called pragmatism has a particularly American face, having been associated first with the work of John Dewey and William James at the turn of the twentieth century and later reemerging in the neopragmatism of my friend and former teacher Richard Rorty, who passed away in 2007. When I look at some of the interviews Rorty gave during his last years, I don't think he was very optimistic about the future of his country and its place in the world. I don't think he would have believed the United States would so quickly throw off its experimentation with radical Republican politics and embrace a reenergized Democratic Party, as appeared to be the case in 2008. I think he would have expected even less that that party would come under the leadership of Obama, although Obama's Democratic Party resembles in many ways the kind of politics that Rorty would have desired for his country.

In an interview given soon after George Bush won the presidency in 2000 Rorty called the return to the White House of the Republican Party "a true disaster, for the US and for the world. The new administration will spend money that should be spent on the poor on absurd and dangerous projects . . . and the religious right, which is a truly dangerous and potentially fascist movement, will be greatly strengthened. I see no bright side to the next four years." He also went on to affirm the Democratic Party as "the only viable means for progressive politics in the US" but seemed resigned, as many progressives have been in the years since he gave that interview, to a political spectrum dominated by the Republican Party. As he put it, "I cannot explain the failure of the American electorate to rise above selfishness and greed. I wish I could. My country has enjoyed unparalleled power and wealth for a decade, and has not used either its power or its wealth to decrease human suffering. It seems to me a great tragedy." Finally, when asked if the twenty-first century will also be an American century, and how the Unites States can help to make the world more humane, Rorty sounded a truly dismal note:

> The US could do what it did under President Carter—say that human rights around the world were the chief priority of American foreign policy—and then actually act on this conviction. The US can't bring peace and democracy to the world all by itself, but it could do a lot by setting a good example. I do not think there is any hope of this happening, so I see no reason to think that the twenty-first will be an American century. The century will probably see the US displaced by China as the most powerful nation, and this will probably mean that world leadership will switch from a democracy to a dictatorship. We shall go from a leading nation that provides a not very good example to one that provides a really awful example.

Rorty lived to see much of the world he foresaw start coming to fruition. He saw 9/11 and the aftermath; he saw the Bush administration's bungled projects in Iraq and failure to act from New Orleans to Darfur. He saw the nightmare visions of Abu Ghraib and the justifiable outrage they provoked around the world. He saw all this, and he

must have seen Obama's speech at the 2004 convention, his rallying cry against a politics that sees a red America and a blue America
instead of the United States of America. He would have known of
Obama's candidacy, declared in the winter of 2007; but he was at that
time already dying of pancreatic cancer, which had been diagnosed
the previous summer and which ultimately took his life in June of
that year, a full year and a half before Obama's historic victory, and
long before Obama would have been anything other than a long-shot
candidate of the antiwar left.

And yet, as one blogger has noted, "Richard Rorty's 1998 work
Achieving Our Country reads like the master plan of Barack Obama's
successful presidential election campaign." In many ways, Obama's
rapid rise to power over the year and a half after Rorty's death represents the very political turn that Rorty hoped for and despaired
of in equal measure. This is true in part because, as the blogger
described it, the politician put into practice the philosopher's vision
for "a reconfiguration of the American left" away from a politics of
spectatorship in which left-leaning philosophers proffer cynical criticisms of the status quo without venturing practical solutions. But this
reconfiguration is deeper than a mere move from passive critique to
active engagement in politics. Rorty would have approved of Obama's
politics because they represent the most effective likely path toward
reducing suffering in the world. And the reason they do so is because,
unlike both the Republicans who had held power for so much of
recent memory and the idealistic left that opposed them, Obama's
politics are pragmatic at the core, driven by results in the real world
as opposed to principles in an ideal one.

My motivation in turning to the 2008 election and the Obama
presidency is to make a point about the fundamentalism of everyday life and how it works in terms of politics and ultimately human
rights. The Democratic Party that took over the presidency after eight
years of Republican domination did not replace right-wing fundamentalism with left-wing fundamentalism. Under Obama's influence it replaced a political and religious fundamentalism with political pragmatism and, it's fair to say, religious moderation. As Obama
has written in telling the story of his conversion to Christianity, which
came about, as he phrased it, "as a choice and not an epiphany,"

Almost by definition, faith and reason operate in different domains and involve different paths to discerning truth. Reason—and science—involves the accumulation of knowledge based on realities we can all apprehend. Religion, by contrast, is based on truths that are not provable through ordinary human understanding—the "belief in things not seen." When science teachers insist on keeping creationism or intelligent design out of their classrooms, they are not asserting that scientific knowledge is superior to religious insight. They are simply insisting that each path to knowledge involves different rules and that those rules are not interchangeable.

Obama's take on the relation between religion and science is the hallmark of moderate faith. It depends on the idea that there are different kinds of belief that can coexist without coming into conflict. But what does the fact of the president's moderate faith mean for his policies, in particular for the question of how human rights will fare with U.S. foreign policy under his leadership? As of this writing, Obama's record has been mixed. While he has openly renounced the use of torture on terror suspects and set a time line for closing Guantánamo, the practice of extraordinary rendition apparently continues, and Guantánamo remains open, with no solution in sight for the remaining detainees. Is this failure of progress due to Obama's pragmatism, his refusal to fully embrace principled positions, or to the deadlocked political culture of Washington? And if he is a pragmatist at the core, what would a pragmatist theory of human rights look like in the first place?

In some senses, the very notion of human rights appears to rest on that most unpragmatic of foundations, namely, a truth, ideal, or principle. "We hold these truths to be self-evident," reads the famous opening line of the second paragraph of the American Declaration of Independence, "that all men are created equal, that they are endowed by their Creator with certain unalienable Rights, that among these are Life, Liberty and the pursuit of Happiness." This very concept and almost the very same words crown the opening lines of the United Nations' Universal Declaration of Human Rights, adopted and proclaimed by the General Assembly on December 10, 1948, that "recognition of the inherent dignity and of the equal and inalienable rights of all members of the human family is the foundation of freedom, justice and peace in the world."

"Inherent," "inalienable," "created," "endowed by their Creator": these are all expressions that pragmatists find at best philosophically unjustified and at worst potentially damaging. Why philosophically unjustified? To begin with, pragmatists would argue, there is nothing inherent or indeed inalienable about a right of any kind. A right is always bestowed on an individual or group by some sovereign power. Being so bestowed, it is always alienable. Indeed, the mere fact that there is a need for a Universal Declaration of Human Rights is demonstration of the extremely alienable nature of human rights. What the declaration means to say, then, is that we, the representatives of those sovereign nations gathered here, believe and affirm that these rights *should* be inalienable, that we *should* treat all humans *as if* these rights were inherent. While this may sound like mere intellectual quibbling, the pragmatist's position is that the imposition of absolute goals based on the positing of real essences such as inherent or inalienable rights can actually hamper the piecemeal improvement of people's conditions in real life.

Here is how Rorty confronted a question posed to him about proposals for reparations to be paid to American blacks for the two hundred years of slavery their forefathers were subjected to:

> These are valid and serious arguments, but there are also valid and serious arguments for taxing the citizens of the First World down to the standard of living of the average inhabitant of the Third World, and distributing the proceeds of this taxation to the latter. But since neither set of arguments will lead to any such action being taken, I am not sure how much time we should spend thinking about them, as opposed to thinking about measures that have some chance of actually being carried out. It would be better to think about what might actually be done than to think about what an absolutely perfect world would look like. The best can be the enemy of the better.

This last, pithy formulation, which has become a mantra of the Obama administration, contains in it the pragmatist's main reservation concerning a discourse centered on inherent and inalienable rights. There are a variety of ways in which the best can be the enemy of the better, in which insistence on inviolable principles can hamper actual improvement. In the realm of rights, the insistence on inviolable principle might serve as justification for unilateral action and for violence over diplomacy, which could lead to a sum increase in suffering instead of a decrease, for example. Here I am thinking of the reference to human rights used by the Bush administration as one of its arguments in selling the Iraq War to the American public. Indeed, self-proclaimed liberal critics of religious extremism such as Sam Harris and Christopher Hitchens not only supported the Iraq invasion and the overall war on terror on the basis of such argumentation but have both also argued for the permissibility of torture in hypothetical cases in which the suspect or detainee might have information that would, again hypothetically, save lives and hence reduce suffering.

Here, then, is the paradox. What appears to be the flexible, pragmatic position (permitting torture in cases where it might reduce suffering for others) actually results from a principled position (such tactics are justified because they are the means to a end that is itself the greater principle). In other words, once you accept the inviolability of a principle, it can always be trumped by an even more inviolable principle. Furthermore, this entire motivational structure rests on an implicit belief in the code of codes that provides a kind of ultimate justification for violence against others. Belief in the code of codes is written into the very language of the Universal Declaration of Human Rights when it says that rights are inherent, or in the Declaration of Independence when it states that humans are endowed with these rights by their Creator. The idea behind both propositions is that rights are in some sense written in a language deeper than ephemeral reality, that they are inscribed into the very being of nature. Obviously the latter formulation, written by the deist Thomas Jefferson, does not try to hide the reference to the origin of such an endowment: the Creator. While the Universal Declaration avoids such an overt attribution, positing rights as inherent begs the question of endowment.

Furthermore, the all-important article 1 of the declaration—"All human beings are born free and equal in dignity and rights. They are endowed with reason and conscience and should act towards one another in a spirit of brotherhood"—uses the language of endowment and makes the startlingly counterfactual claim that all human beings are born free and equal in dignity and rights. If this is not to be taken as simply absurd at face value, then it must be in reference to some ideal as opposed to factual birth. For as we all know, in a factual sense, practically no one is born free and equal in dignity and rights.

But why make such a fuss about the language of human rights? Isn't it just mean-spirited to pick away at a declaration that clearly intends nothing but good for the world? The problem, again, with the language of endowment and creation is that it presupposes rights as something found in human nature and not made. In presupposing this given nature of rights, it further implies that human knowledge has access to these rights as to some writing or ultimate law, a code underlying all temporal, culturally specific codes that would correspond to the way things are in themselves. When a person or a nation believes they have that kind of knowledge, it is not a far stretch for them to believe themselves justified in almost any action in defense of the principles they read in such a code. The pragmatist's concern is that such certainty is more likely to lead to violence and suffering than would a humble and pragmatic commitment to merely bettering things.

My good friend Kevin Jon Heller is a professor of law at the University of Melbourne, and as an expert on international criminal law he has served as a consultant to Radovan Karadzic in his trial for war crimes in the International Criminal Tribunal for the former Yugoslavia. As Kevin would and does tell anyone who wishes to know, he does work like this in part because the right to the best possible defense is a fundamental human right and hence one that should be available to anyone, no matter what we feel about him or her. Obviously I agree. But one of the problems with justifying the defense of human rights on the basis of their inherence in some human essence is that we naturally chafe at the idea that different people who have acted in different ways really are, when it comes to it, deserving of the same rights. Hence something in our being may scream out at the notion that a perpetrator of genocide or crimes against humanity is deserving of having his rights protected when he has so grossly violated those of so many others. When we see the right to the best defense as a mere pragmatic extension of the legal principles we have agreed upon for the determination of guilt or innocence in a democratic society, however, it becomes clear that someone like Karadzic must have the best possible defense not because he implicitly deserves it in any way but because the outcome, his being tried and possibly convicted for the crimes he has committed, entirely requires it. In other words, our very designation of someone as a war criminal depends on the due process protected by the notion of human rights, the very due process that the Bush administration so flagrantly skirted by designating a priori anyone in detention as an "enemy combatant." If you are in Guantánamo, goes the reasoning, you must be guilty, since you are, after all, in Guantánamo.

The final philosophical objection to the presumption of a founding principle for human rights is the limitations produced by any such principle. Once rights have been extended to "all members of the human family," as the declaration puts it, this immediately begins to beg the question of who fits into this family and whether those deemed not worthy of the designation of human are also justified claimants to the rights with which we claim to be endowed. Will "higher" life forms eventually be included? Do group identities demand a special protection as well as do individuals? Are certain groups de facto excluded from the current wording? Article 16 of the Universal Declaration, concerning marriage and the family, is problematic in this regard:

(1) Men and women of full age, without any limitation due to race, nationality or religion, have the right to marry and to found a family. They are entitled to equal rights as to marriage, during marriage and at its dissolution. (2) Marriage shall be entered into only with the free and full consent of the intending spouses. (3) The family is the natural and fundamental group unit of society and is entitled to protection by society and the State.

While part 2 protects anyone from the slavery and repression of forced marriage, part 1 can be read as limiting marriage to heterosexual couples, and part 3 entitles states to protect the nuclear family—and thus, one might assume, discriminate against nonnuclear or nontraditional families—on the basis of its "natural and fundamental" status.

The dangers of phrasing rights in terms of their natural, inherent, or endowed status are thus quite real. What is the alternative? Were human rights to be conceptualized as they are in fact deployed, that is, pragmatically, they would be understood to refer not to inherent principles of human nature but to actual agreements among sovereign bodies. While they might be limited in time and place, there would be no illusion about this limitation, and hence the extension of rights to new claimants could not be hindered by the presumption of their ideal nature. Granted, further limitation of those rights could not be hindered in principle; but the pragmatist would argue that there is nothing in the principle itself hindering their further limitation right now. If governments wish to limit rights, they tend to do so, and in the unlikely event that the United Nations would meet again sometime soon with the express purpose of restricting the applicability of human rights, there is nothing about the principled nature of those rights that could stop that from happening, just as nothing about the principled nature of rights ever stopped them from being violated prior to the Universal Declaration.

The key point of a pragmatist theory of human rights, then, is to take into account the fact that all human thought, all human agency, no matter how selfless or oriented toward ideals it might be, still emerges from a given cultural and political context and takes implicit beliefs from that context. Thus all political thought is inevitably "ethnocentric" to some extent and, here's the rub, this ethnocentric character should not for that reason alone invalidate it—because, of course, this character is an inevitable condition of all thought. There can be no idea of a universal justice, for example, but only of a justice conceived of as what Rorty once called an ever-widening circle of loyalty: one begins loyal to one's family and friends, then nation, then to other nations sharing one's view, and then perhaps to some notion of humanity taken as one, and then on to who knows what. But the process is inextricably rooted in that home self and the soup of ideas it grew up in.

Obama's positions and voting record in the Senate demonstrated that his values are progressive. But the change he has talked about has always been, from the beginning, an embrace of pragmatism over ideology. Take his stand on abortion: "Yes, I am in favor of protecting a woman's right to choose, but no matter what your firm beliefs are on this issue, beliefs I respect and understand, surely we can agree to do everything we can to prevent unwanted pregnancies in the first place." Such an approach eschews any discussion about the "truth" of whether a fetus is a human life or not and sticks to formulating a common goal in pragmatic terms. This approach has characterized his writings and speeches on foreign policy and specifically on human rights as well.

As the *New York Times* reported in an article in late 2008 on the challenge Obama faced in naming a CIA head, "In a speech last year, Mr. Obama cast the matter as a practical issue, as well as a moral one. 'We cannot win a war unless we maintain the high ground and keep the people on our side,' he said. 'But because the administration decided to take the low road, our troops have more enemies.'" This is not a new form of rationalization. In every instance I can find in Obama's writings, he places concern for human rights, for alleviating suffering around the world, for working in tandem with other nations as opposed to unilaterally alongside and in the context of preservation of national interests and U.S. power.

For example, in discussing multilateralism and the importance of international institutions, Obama has written as follows:

> No country has a bigger stake than we do in strengthening international institutions—which is why we pushed for their creation in the first place, and why we need to take the lead in improving them . . . For those who chafe at the prospect of working with our allies to solve the pressing global challenges we face, let me suggest at least one area where we can act unilaterally and improve our standing in the world—by perfecting our own democracy and leading by example . . . When we detain

suspects without trial or ship them off in the dead of night to countries where we know they'll be tortured, we weaken our ability to press for human rights and the rule of law in despotic regimes . . . This unwillingness to make hard choices and live up to our own ideals doesn't just undermine U.S. credibility in the eyes of the world. It undermines the U.S. government's credibility with the American people.

Does Obama believe in human rights? Of this there can be no doubt. But it is extremely telling that he persists in couching almost every reference to them in pragmatic terms. Yes, pressing for human rights is an end in itself, he says, but then he immediately follows this by arguing that failure to live up to one's ideals weakens credibility at home and abroad. The truth is, for Obama the two sides are inextricably entangled. The very ideals for which a government even exists, the ideals that drive his own work in government, themselves also serve the interests of that government's efficacy.

Obama elsewhere quotes John F. Kennedy as saying, "To those people in the huts and villages of half the globe struggling to break the bonds of mass misery, we pledge our best efforts to help them help themselves, for whatever period is required—not because the Communists may be doing it, not because we seek their votes, but because it is right. If a free society cannot help the many who are poor, it cannot save the few who are rich." We should not miss how Kennedy himself could not avoid encasing his reference to an absolute value within the pragmatic language of means—in this case, the self-preservation of the rich. I do not mean to be cynical in noticing this, and Obama was far from being cynical in citing it. As he goes on to write, "Forty-five years later, that mass misery still exists. If we are to fulfill Kennedy's promise—and serve our long-term security interests—then we will have to go beyond a more prudent use of military force. We will have to align our policies to help reduce the spheres of insecurity, poverty, and violence around the world, and give more people a stake in the global order that has served us so well."

Abiding by international law, respecting and promoting human rights: of course these are important goals, but maintaining them as pure ideals is neither particularly useful nor even the best way of promoting them. "Why conduct ourselves in this way?" Obama asks,

> because nobody benefits more than we do from the observance of international rules of the road. We can't win converts to those rules if we act as if they applied to everyone but us. When the world's sole superpower willingly restrains its power and abides by internationally agreed-upon standards of conduct, it sends a message that these are rules worth following, and robs terrorists and dictators of the argument that these rules are simply tools of American imperialism.

In politics, in the pursuit of human rights, just as in science, we can do perfectly well without the false sense of stability and purpose provided by the code of codes. It is the active ingredient of all everyday fundamentalisms, whether we find them to be noxious or beneficial. If we can wean ourselves from depending on it for social goods we can foster just as well without it, then perhaps we can learn to spot it in those other cases as well. Far from being an enemy in this endeavor, religions have often led the way in revealing and undermining the pretensions of the code of codes. The next chapter explores the history of that religious attitude, alongside that of the religious fundamentalism that has been its nemesis.

3 The Language of God

Plato's Uncertainty

I remember seeing the previews for the movie *The Matrix* when it was released in the summer of 1999. I was living with my wife in a cottage we rented not far from Stanford University, where I was about to finish my PhD and move on to a new job and new life. Like many of our friends we were intrigued by the snippets of stylized martial arts we saw on the television screen, and by the ubiquitous advertising campaign inviting the curious to visit the film's Web site with the question, what is the Matrix?

In our case our friends who saw it before us were generous about not spoiling the surprise. We learned what the Matrix was at the moment and in exactly the way the filmmakers intended us to: when Morpheus, played by Laurence Fishburne, offers Keanu Reeve's character, Neo, the choice of two pills, a blue one that will put him to sleep and allow him to convince himself that what has happened was nothing but a dream and a red one that will reveal the truth, that will let him see, in Morpheus's words, how deep the rabbit hole goes.

Naturally, Neo takes the red pill, and the rest is cinematic history. Just as we did, legions of moviegoers thrilled to the sensation of losing their moorings. The reality of Neo's world, which we had just spent the first part of the movie accepting as real, slipped away and was revealed to be the effect of a massive virtual reality program controlling the minds of all humans other than a score of courageous resistance fighters intent on winning humanity's freedom back from the machines that had enslaved us and turned us into compliant sources of energy.

While the premise was shaky, to say the least (as scientists were quick to point out, raising humans to harvest them for their energy would be absurdly inefficient given that the human body requires more energy to live than it ever produces), the cinematic effect clearly struck a chord. What happened was that the Wachowski brothers, the film's directors, successfully translated into cinematic format one of the oldest, most compelling motifs of civilization: the idea that the world as we know it is a dream, a facade, an illusion, and that the truth is out there in another form, waiting to be discovered.

The most influential and time-tested version of this motif is Plato's "cave allegory" from book VII of his dialogue *The Republic*. In this dialogue Socrates describes the ideal role philosophers should play in government by telling the story of a society whose members all live in a cave, bound and immobile, with a fire lit behind them and their eyes all facing the cave's wall. Socrates argues that for these men, who have never seen anything else, the world is composed exclusively of the shadows thrown up on the wall of the cave. If one man managed to escape and leave the confines of the cave, he would at first be blinded by the sunlight; when he finally returned to tell the others of his discovery, they would mock him and even ultimately kill him should he try to convince them of the truth:

> And before his eyes had recovered—and the adjustment would not be quick—while his vision was still dim, if he had to compete again with the perpetual prisoners in recognizing the shadows, wouldn't he invite ridicule? Wouldn't it be said of him that he'd returned from his upward journey with his eyesight ruined and that it isn't worthwhile even to try to travel upward? And, as for anyone who tried to free them and lead them upward, if they could somehow get their hands on him, wouldn't they kill him?

Plato's ultimate point in situating the allegory in the seventh book of his dialogue on the idea of justice would seem to be that there are a few individuals with the perspicacity to discover the truth of the world, and that such men should be entrusted with the management of society. But more powerful than his argument for a kind of benign totalitarianism is the image his analogy passed down to successive generations, the image of a world hiding behind the one we actually inhabit, whose truth can be known by a select few.

The Matrix is only a relatively recent and striking example from a series of interpretations of this image of the world that have at their core the notion that the real world, the one hiding behind our shadow world of illusions, consists of a kind of knowledge, a master code determining every aspect of our lives, but which only a very few can ever hope to read. The implications should be clear: if you believe in this image and feel you are one of the few who have mastered that code, or even that the pathway you have chosen in life will lead to that knowledge, or that the people you have identified as your mentors have access to it, then there will be very little common ground on which to arbitrate differences you may have with those who do not share your belief in that code.

In Plato's story, perhaps foreshadowing Socrates' own condemnation and execution years later, it is the philosopher who has seen the truth who is ultimately persecuted and killed by those who fail to see. And yet it is no stretch to see how a society that earnestly believes it has arrived at such a truth, and that the rest of the world labors under dangerous illusions, could take justice into its own hands and defend its vision of the truth with force. Socrates, however, softens the certainty of his own vision with an important caveat. Here is how he interprets his story to Glaucon:

> The whole image, Glaucon, must be fitted with what we said before. The visible realm should be likened to the prison dwelling, and the light of the fire inside it to the power of the sun. And if you interpret the upward journey and the study of things above as the upward journey of the soul to the intelligible realm, you'll grasp what I hope to convey, since that is what you wanted to hear about. Whether it's true or not, only the god knows.

In a dialogue in which Plato expounds Socrates' theory of the truth as hiding beyond or above the visible world, accessible to only a select few, he also freely admits that he cannot know for sure if this very vision itself is the true one. In other words, the accessibility of that special knowledge is so questionable that one never really knows if one has it or not.

While attention to this brief note of uncertainty in Socrates' speech may seem disproportionate, it fully corresponds to the general tenor of Plato's theory of truth. While the philosopher indeed propagated the idea of truth, beauty, and justice as eternal, unchanging forms, his approach to these issues through the voice of his teacher and protagonist, Socrates, tended to be cautious, tentative, and humble. Although such humility may simply have been a characteristic of Socrates and his teaching style—and may have been more rhetorical than authentic on his part—ultimately we can see how the very theory demanded it. For a theory of hidden truths always raises the specter that the truth one claims to lay hold of may itself be yet another shadow dancing on the cave wall.

Plato was intrigued by the question of what form our knowledge of the world would take were it to be true knowledge. In his dialogue *Cratylus* he describes a debate between Hermogenes, Cratylus, and Socrates about the nature of language: do words mean what they mean because they accurately reflect the world, or do they do so because of an arbitrary and conventional relation to the things they name? Toward the end of the debate, after interrogating each of his friends on their views, Socrates outlines a view that will be of enormous influence to Western thought: it is ultimately unimportant whether language is like what it signifies or unlike it, since one way or the other it is removed from reality itself and hence unlikely to lead us to the truth. As he says,

> If it's really the case that one can learn about things through names and that one can also learn about them through themselves, which would be the better and clearer way to learn about them? Is it better to learn from the likeness both whether it itself is a good likeness and also the truth it is a likeness of? Or is it better to learn from the truth both the truth itself and also whether the likeness of it is properly made?

Faced with the question of how well language can represent the truth, then, Socrates points to the possibility that the truth can be known, not via a language or other such instrument but in itself. But it is important to note, again, that this claim remains a *possibility* for Socrates. As the dialogue concludes with Socrates and Cratylus exploring what knowledge would be like were it not subject to the vagaries and inconsistencies of the language we use to represent it, Socrates yet again cautions against the temptation of certainty: "It's certainly possible that things are that way, Cratylus, but it's also possible that they are not. So you must investigate them courageously and thoroughly and not accept anything easily."

Can there be knowledge of the world beyond the senses we use to learn about it or the languages we speak to communicate about it? Plato's philosophy simultaneously evinces hope for an affirmative answer to this question and skepticism as to its possibility. The image his thought bequeathed of a world of illusions that hide from us an ultimate truth has been perhaps the single most powerful motif in Western culture. It has influenced both the religions that have held so much of Western culture in their sway and the practices of exploration and analysis that led to the scientific revolution and the modern industrial West.

There can be no doubt that the majority of both religious and scientific thinkers who have been influenced by this model have been guided by the hope for that ultimate knowledge. The problem with such hope is that, if not accompanied by a healthy skepticism as to its possibility as well as humility concerning one's own access to it, it can promote the attitude toward truth that I have called fundamentalism. This is in no way to suggest that all fundamentalisms are inspired by Plato. Nevertheless, the Abrahamic religions, or religions of the book, whose conflicts and cohabitations were central to European intellectual and political history, have all had access to this image and have incorporated it in one way or another into their respective traditions. Furthermore, as I just mentioned, the rationalist tradition that led to the emergence of scientific modernity and secular humanism not only was also influenced by this image but also grew out of the very religious traditions that it would later denounce for their failure to cast off the blinders of dogma.

Ultimately, as I try to show in this chapter, resistance to dogma cannot be painted as the work of a rationalist tradition against the unreasoning dictates of faith. Rather, the skeptical attitude toward the possibility of an ultimate truth that was already present in Plato infected the religious traditions he influenced with a tenacity that would not let go. Whenever and wherever people have thought deeply about the relation of human knowledge to God, this profound uncertainty has emerged and reasserted itself. And it has been this very uncertainty that has repeatedly undermined dogma and made way for the progress of knowledge. But while opposed to dogma and necessary for science, uncertainty is not the enemy of faith; rather, those traditions that recognized and developed a separation between what one can know and learn through the senses and the sorts of total questions that transcend the limits of knowledge were more conducive to the progress of science and reason than those that held on to the hope for absolute truth. In a parallel way, to the extent that the rationalist tradition itself failed to heed the lessons of Plato's uncertainty, it smuggled into its own pursuits the very addiction to dogma that risks stultifying knowledge and opening the doors to intolerance and violence. Science emerged from faith because faith came to know its own limits; without the same humility, there is nothing to stop the noble pursuit of knowledge from degenerating into a servile protector of power, wealth, or whatever ideology rules the day.

God's Tongue

Plato's ideas about the hidden nature of truth and how we might or might not come to know it made their way into the Abrahamic religious traditions via the writings of the third-century Greek philosopher Plotinus. In his *Enneads* he transmits the ideas of his teacher, Ammonius Saccas, with whom he studied philosophy in the ancient Egyptian capital of Alexandria. In the *Enneads* Plotinus develops the Platonic idea of the One as origin and truth of all being, which is itself beyond being and ungraspable by the intellect. Many scholars locate in this position the origin of what is known as apophatic, or negative, theology, the doctrine that the best that human intelligence can muster is to describe what God is not, as opposed to what he is.

But it would be a mistake to assume that there are two easily distinguishable theological traditions, one accustomed to making positive statements about the accessibility of God's will to human knowledge and the other denying that possibility. Rather, what Plotinus's insight brought to the religious traditions that incorporated his thought was an awareness of how tenuous human knowledge of the divine must be. In other words, any theology of revelation that followed him would at least have to be attentive to the possibility that such revealed knowledge would transcend the human ability to understand it, an insight that would eventually lead to the separation of faith and intellect by such a canonical theologian as Thomas Aquinas. Thus did uncertainty as to the ultimate nature of things make its way into Western religious discourse, despite the assurances we are often given, from the perspective of Enlightenment modernity, that prior to the advent of modern secular humanism, in Mark Lilla's words, "Christian theologians . . . took their assertions to be absolutely true on the basis of reason and revelation."

If the idea of an ultimate truth so alien to the human intellect that it might be inaccessible made its way into Western thought through Plotinus, so did Plato's idea of what that ultimate knowledge might look like. His notion that the things of the world might in a sense speak their own language deeply impressed one of the early Church's most influential thinkers, Saint Augustine, the fourth-century theologian and philosopher who converted to Christianity and became the bishop of Hippo, in present-day Algeria. The idea that the Truth can be read in itself, independently of the natural languages we use to express it, was central to Augustine's belief that the world is a book written by God's own finger in a language not of words but, as Umberto Eco has put it, of things themselves. The complex practice of biblical hermeneutics that emerged from Augustine's teaching, through which the scriptures are read and interpreted on four different levels, owed much to this idea. For if the things of the world are themselves a language, to read that language and understand the world one has to discover its code.

Augustine's metaphor of the world as a kind of divine book resurfaced powerfully in the sixteenth century with some of the earliest scientific thinkers. These scientists believed, like Augustine, that the world contained secrets that could be revealed only through study and interpretation, and while their descendants would by and large forgo the analogy to biblical hermeneutics, these men openly described their investigations of the natural world as a search to understand the word of God.

I just wrote "by and large" in the sentence above because, in fact, while open analogies between scientific discovery and biblical exegesis have lost their broad appeal, some cases still exist. Take the best-selling *The Language of God*, by the remarkable and tenacious geneticist Francis Collins, who led the team that in 1997 announced the completion of the Human Genome Project. A world-class scientist whose hard work and perseverance are in part responsible for the fact that the 3-billion-codon-long human genetic sequence is now in the public domain, Collins is also a devout Christian and has written a book in which he argues that his commitment to science and to God are perfectly compatible.

The basic idea of his argument is clear and widely known: in uncovering the genetic code we have discovered the book of life, the book "written in the DNA language by which God spoke life into being." "Yes," he goes on to qualify, "it is written in a language we understand very poorly, and it will take decades, if not centuries, to understand its implications, but we had crossed a one-way bridge into profoundly new territory."

What are the stakes of engaging in this metaphor, if indeed it is a metaphor? While significantly more up-to-date, perhaps, than claiming that the language of God is an arcane form of Hebrew or even Gaelic, does labeling DNA the language of God do anything other than help a scientist in his personal quest to reconcile faith and knowledge? Here's how Collins spells out the comparison between the genetic code and a language:

Another way to think about this is to consider the metaphor of language. The average educated English speaker has a vocabulary of about 20,000 words. Those words can be used to construct rather simple documents (such as an owner's manual for your car) or much more complex works of literature such as

James Joyce's *Ulysses*. In the same way, worms, insects, fish, and birds apparently need an extensive vocabulary of 20,000 genes to function, though they use these resources in less elaborate ways than we do.

Aside from the unwarranted assumption that a vehicle owner's manual is simple, this explanation strikes me as cogent and useful. The genome is more than 3 billion codons long, spread across twenty-four chromosomes. The vocabulary of the genome consists of the some thirty thousand genes used to write "the book." These "words" are composed of different combinations in differing lengths of the four base pairs, or letters, of the genetic alphabet. But for all its illustrative value, where does God fit in the metaphor? English is a natural language, so unless you are assuming that it was also written by God—which sort of takes the bite out of your claim for DNA—the analogy with English does nothing for the language of God thesis.

The motif of the language of God has inhabited the scientific investigation of the world since long before the onset of the scientific method, and while it shows up in more obvious forms in such openly religious scientists as Francis Collins, it also informs how even die-hard atheists like Richard Dawkins see the task of science, as I argued in the first chapter. But while science has often, if innocently, embraced the logic of the world as code as a heuristic in its quest for understanding, religions have often been more skeptical about the human ambition to grasp the kind of knowledge of the universe that could be described as the language of God.

According to the Old Testament, the natural tongues of men descended from the great confusion created by God to punish men for their hubris in trying to build the Tower of Babel. The assumption among many medieval scholars was that the differences among natural languages as well as the internal inconsistencies and indeterminacies of each could have resulted only from their having degenerated from the language that Adam had first spoken when addressed by God. While a majority identified Hebrew as having the most direct lineage to the language of God, Umberto Eco has uncovered other instances of scholars advancing similar claims for their own languages. Perhaps the most amusing of such cases was made for

Gaelic, for which seventh-century Irish grammarians affirmed that "in the tower [of Babel] there were only nine materials and . . . these were clay and water, wool and blood, wood and lime, pitch, linen, and bitumen . . . These represent noun, pronoun, verb, adverb, participle, conjunction, preposition, interjection." Gaelic, then, being the first made of the languages after Babel, could ensure its connection to the true language prior to Babel—when words and things were identical—and it could do so because its grammar supposedly retained a fundamental connection to the materials of which the tower itself was built.

The idea of the degeneration of human languages from their Edenic unity clearly finds resonance with Plato's notion of languages as faulty representations of the truth of the world. But it was also the notable differences among natural languages that led some theologians to the conclusion that whatever language God speaks, it must be different from the languages of men and ultimately beyond comprehension.

Think how far even this position is from the straw-man believer the atheists need to construct. For their arguments faith can be only a kind of biblical literalism, a belief without evidence in what scripture dictates. And yet already in the fourth century Augustine had dedicated a whole book to arguing that the Bible can and should not be read literally. The entire theological tradition of Christianity, in other words, is founded on the denial of what the atheist critics have attributed to all religion.

As early religious thinkers often noticed, from individual words to sentences to books, concatenations of language often produce astoundingly indeterminate meanings. Ironically, the most ardent promoters of literalist readings of the Bible are also those most likely to forget that the copy they carry around in English is already several translations removed from the original, and that Christ is not and never was Jesus' last name (it's the English pronunciation of the Greek translation of the Hebrew word for messiah, or "anointed one"). The latter assumption was the target of one of the etymologies presented by the seventh-century bishop of Seville, Saint Isidore, and we can read in his discussion of the meaning of God's various names a healthy reminder of the indeterminacy of not only translation but any attempt we might make to know the real will of God.

The tetragrammaton, or mystical name of God, as Isidore writes in book VII of his *Etymologies*, "is called 'ineffable' not because it cannot be spoken but because in no way can it be bounded by human sense and intellect." Further on, criticizing the application of the term *perfect* to God for the implicit requirement that what is perfect has been completed or made, Isidore goes on to concede that the same critique applies to any use of language to speak of God: "But human poverty of diction has taken up this term from our usage, and likewise for the remaining terms, insofar as what is ineffable can be spoken of in any way—for human speech says nothing suitable about God—and so the other terms are also deficient." God, Isidore concludes, can be spoken of only by metaphor or analogy, for we can know only his traces: "They behold his appearance, whose traces they now try to comprehend, that is, him whom it is said they see through a mirror. For in relation to God, position and vesture and place and time are spoken of not properly, but metaphorically, by way of analogy." What we can know, in other words, through our language are the appearances of God, his reflections, his traces. But knowledge of God or of his thought, will, or intention is not only accidentally and temporarily beyond human reach but also of a nature fundamentally alien to human knowledge.

The theology of uncertainty was engendered in Christianity in part by Greek philosophy, as I have outlined. But Plotinus's writings were enormously influential to the Semitic religions as well. In fact, the philosophy, theology, and scientific practices developed during the Middle Ages in Europe would not have been possible had it not been for the translation of Greek thought by Muslim and Jewish scholars and its preservation in the libraries of Islamic Spain and elsewhere. Despite the profound antagonism between Christians, Jews, and Muslims characterizing the Mediterranean world of the Middle Ages as much as ours today, the Christian, Jewish, and Islamic intellectual and theological traditions exercised enormous influence on one another.

Unlike with Christian theology, Jewish interpretive practices resisted being codified into the doctrinal sources of rival versions of the faith. Instead, different techniques of reading and interpreting the Torah circulated in the form of the mystical practice of kabbalah, from the Hebrew word for "tradition." Key to the kabbalistic tradition is the very idea I have been exploring, that creation itself can be seen as a kind of language. According to one early kabbalistic treatise, the *Sefer Yetzirah* (Book of Creation), God created the universe out of a set number of stones that are simultaneously the letters of the Hebrew alphabet and the ten Sefirot, the enumeration of God's possible manifestation. From the various combinations of these letters and metaphysical levels, the book teaches that the apparently infinite variety of existence can be generated by the combination of a finite number of letters and numbers: "Two stones build two houses, three stones build six houses, four stones build twenty-four houses, five stones build a hundred and twenty houses, six stones build seven hundred and twenty houses, seven stones build five thousand and forty houses. Begin from there and think of what the mouth is unable to say and the ear unable to hear."

As is apparent, the kabbalistic view of language comes close to the Platonic notion of a kind of knowledge of things themselves, from which we might assume that Jewish interpretive practices would in fact favor and propagate the idea of a kind of master code underlying all of existence. However, what we see in both kabbalistic texts and the mainstream Jewish theological tradition is an emphasis on the incompatibility between whatever wisdom one may achieve through kabbalistic practice, on the one hand, and practical or scientific knowledge of the world on the other. According to the Lurianic tradition of kabbalah, for example, which is attributed to the sixteenth-century mystic Isaac Luria, the interpretability of texts and the combinatory power of kabbalah undermine even the assumption of God's own knowledge as complete. As one commentator has said, "At the heart of Luria's teachings is the imperfection of beginning. Existence does not begin with a perfect Creator bringing into being an imperfect universe; rather, the existence of the universe is the result of an inherent flaw or crisis within the infinite Godhead, and the purpose of creation is to correct it." The thirteenth-century Spanish kabbalist Abraham Abulafia, for his part, while believing that the original language must coincide perfectly with creation as opposed to merely representing it, nonetheless held that the secrets of the kabbalah would never be revealed in their entirety until the end of time.

While his version of kabbalah was highly idiosyncratic, Abulafia was nevertheless deeply influenced by his countryman the Jewish doctor and theologian Moses Maimonides, whose *Guide for the Perplexed* is still considered one of the primary texts of apophatic theology. Born in Córdoba in the early twelfth century, Maimonides' family was forced to flee and eventually moved to Morocco, when the Almohades dynasty from northern Africa took over Andalusia and forced all its inhabitants to convert to Islam or leave. A great reader of Greek philosophy as well as of Plotinus, Maimonides was in turn an influence on the Christian scholastic philosophers, including Aquinas, even if scholasticism in general did not accept the prohibition on saying anything positive about God.

Maimonides wrote his *Guide* to, in his own words, "enlighten a religious man" who is "lost in perplexity and anxiety" because his "moral and religious duties" have come into conflict with "his philosophical studies." Because this religious man is convinced of the reasonableness of the truths he learns through science, "he finds it difficult to accept as correct the teaching based on the literal interpretation of the Law [the Torah]." The problem thus stated, Maimonides slides quickly into the solution: we must interpret the Torah and the Midrashim based on an understanding of words as *homonyms*, as having more than one meaning. In other words, we fail to make scripture compatible with science because we assume scripture to be *the* language as opposed to *a* language. We assume it to have the status of the code of codes, where every word signifies exactly one aspect of the world, and there is only one word for each aspect. But no language has that status. Theology comes into the picture because it is at the theological level that the critique of the code of codes can ultimately get traction. Language pragmatically deployed within contexts seldom runs into its inherent limitations. Words seem to disregard their homonymic limitations and end up doing a fine job of more or less unambiguously defining objects of cognition. The universe in its totality, however, is not an object of cognition, nor could it ever be. Cognition, like perception and reporting in language, takes place in space and time and has no ability whatsoever to make judgments outside space and time.

For theologians like Maimonides, God is a name for a totality, for something ungraspable, for a creative force that cannot be tamed by the human intellect. "The Torah speaks according to the language of man," he quotes, going on to gloss, "that is to say, expressions, which can easily be comprehended and understood by all, are applied to the Creator. Hence the description of God by attributes implying corpore-ality, in order to express His existence; because the multitude of peo-ple do not easily conceive existence unless in connection with a body." He makes his point clearer by bringing together the sublime and the absurd. Most people would not deny God the ability to move, but they might shy away from the idea of the Creator sitting down for a nice plate of pasta and a glass of Chianti. "In fact," Maimonides points out, "it makes no difference whether we ascribe to God eating and drink-ing or locomotion; but according to human modes of expression, that is to say, according to common notions, eating and drinking would be an imperfection in God, while motion would not, in spite of the fact that the necessity of locomotion is the result of some want."

The atheist, the fundamentalist, they both fall prey to the same error. In the theologian's words the error comes from assuming that our knowledge and that of God are of the same nature. "A doubt has been raised, however, of whether His thought includes the infinite. . . . Philosophers . . . have decided that the object of knowledge cannot be a non-existing thing, and that it cannot comprise that which is infinite. Since, therefore, God's knowledge does not admit of any increase, it is impossible that he should know any transient thing." The same logic is applied to static things, and before you know it, God is an idiot. How do we come to this point? By assuming that God knows things in a way similar to how we know things: "The cause of the error of all these schools is their belief that God's knowledge is like ours." If there is a God's-eye view of the world, in other words, it's not anything that we humans could ever make sense of.

But if you think for a moment, that's another way of saying that in matters of metaphysical speculation, we all fall into two camps: agnostics who are aware of being agnostics, and agnostics who think they're something else. These latter agnostics may think they are athe-ists, that is, they may think that they know something certain about the nonexistence of God; or they may be fundamentalists and think that they know something certain about the existence of God and, perhaps more frighteningly, what He wants them to do. But either way they are mistaken. About the sum total of existence as it really is, in itself, we can have only beliefs, not certainty, and to the extent that we understand those beliefs to stem from rich traditions of inquiry that fill our lives with meaning and perhaps lead us to endless questions about the unknown, then all the better.

It is all well and good, one may object, to selectively quote from ancient philosophers, theologians, and poets in order to argue that religion has always been aware of its limitations. But cannot one object that these concerns are marginal? That, in fact, the core doctrine of the major religions is much closer to what the atheist critics claim, that is, to a certainty about beliefs without any evidence? In the case of Catholicism, no Church father is more central to established doctrine than Saint Thomas Aquinas, whose treatises in the thirteenth century were the very epitome of medieval scholasticism. And yet key to Aquinas's understanding of the role of faith is its essential difference from matters of the intellect, that is, its difference from what we understand as knowledge.

For Aquinas, faith is indeed certain; but we must pay attention to how he contrasts the supposed certainty of faith with that of knowledge. Of the three challenges he considers and rejects in the *Summa theologica* to the claim that faith may have a greater certainty than the intellectual virtues, the first is the most all encompassing: while scientific knowledge can be free of doubt about its object, faith often suffers from doubt, and as doubt is to certainty as blackness to whiteness, scientific knowledge must be more certain than faith. While the challenge is strong, it is Aquinas's response that gives us the greatest insight into the relation between faith and knowledge. As he writes, "This doubt is not on the part of the cause of faith, but on our part, in so far as we do not fully grasp matters of faith with our intellect." "Matters of faith," Aquinas argues, "are above the human intellect, while the above three virtues [wisdom, science, and the understanding] are not." In other words, faith can have certitude only in those areas of life that are not subject to our intellect, areas about which we cannot obtain knowledge by dialogue, measurement, or analysis. In the heart of scholastic Christian doctrine, therefore, centuries before

Kant was to impose "limits on knowledge in order to make room for faith," Saint Thomas Aquinas had already separated the two.

In the Christian Middle Ages, the distinctions we naturally make today between specialists in different fields of knowledge simply did not hold. Men of letters included theologians, poets, lawyers, doctors, and mathematicians, and if a man concerned himself with the problems of one discipline, he was very likely to have something to say about most others as well. If this was true of many men, it was markedly true of the fourteenth-century Italian poet Dante Alighieri, in whose works we find the heights of the philosophical, scientific, and theological thought of his day.

In his exercise in historical linguistics, *De vulgari eloquentia* (*Concerning Vernacular Eloquence*), Dante searches beyond and prior to the proliferation of copies of things in natural languages for the very source of those copies and finds there not a word, not even a letter, but merely part of a letter, a consonant, the movement of the larynx that produces the sound *el*. He opposes this name to the first sound an infant makes, a guttural sound he spells "h-e-u" in the original Latin—his transliteration of that cry of pain uttered at the entrance of all humans into earthly existence. When Adam spoke, Dante specifies, he spoke in response to God, which we can stipulate, he goes on to say, "without thereby accepting that God spoke what we would call a language." Rather, Dante explains, as no one can doubt that all that exists bends itself seamlessly to God's will, whatever words Adam heard were produced by the vibrations of the air itself in response to God's ineffable will. Adam's language, therefore, responded to God's question; but this in no way insinuates that God himself speaks a language, the enunciation of which would necessarily imply a limitation in time and place, the articulation of a before and after, a here and there.

Theologians such as Augustine, Maimonides, Isidore, Dante, and Aquinas, men who tried to think their way back though language to the source of being, found time and time again that the point of contact between words and things, between knowledge and being, is lodged in a dimension that refuses all efforts of thought. The irony, therefore, is that none of these explicitly religious thinkers exemplify the fundamentalist logic according to which the ultimate truth of the world can be expressed as a code, accessible to a select few. Isidore and the Church fathers certainly believed in God, but the nature of the God they believed in vetoed in principle any attempt to collapse the difference between the world as appearance and the language of God, a code that could be known independently of time and space, a code that could be known without the limitations of reading and interpretation that all human knowledge requires.

The World as Code

Largely because of the essential role it plays in new technology and media, the term *code* has become one of the most prolific concepts of the late twentieth and twenty-first centuries. The term as we have come to know and use it today is indelibly marked by the context of cybernetics, where it was first used in the mid-1940s in popular and scientific journals to refer to the series of punctures made in a strip of paper that could then be interpreted by the rudimentary computer as instructions for carrying out its task. Soon after, the relatively young field of genetics adopted the term as it sought to understand the process by which certain chemical reactions determined the formation of biological traits. On the basis of Watson and Crick's discovery of the double-helical structure of DNA, geneticists began to discover how the proteins that are the building blocks of more complex biological structures could be produced from a rather simple array of twenty amino acids, themselves encoded by an even simpler series of codons constructed on the basis of four possible nucleotide bases.

Perhaps we should pause to reflect on how different these two contemporary examples of encoding actually are. The encoding of machines involves a deliberate act by a human programmer to create a series of instructions that a machine will follow. The encoding of DNA, which creates a series of instructions that chemical processes follow in constructing living organisms, results from the nondeliberate evolutionary processes of natural selection. Yet the analogy between programming and the creation of life is doubtlessly tempting and has been implicitly and explicitly appropriated by those convinced that the complexity of life offers clear signs of intelligent design.

Let us call the two logics of coding religious and natural, respectively. Under this nomenclature, computer programming would be "religious" not because programmers are like God but because the extrapolation of their task to the cosmic level necessarily invokes the image of a God-like, intelligent creator. The encoding of life at the genetic level, on the other hand, is "natural" insofar as the basic assumption of evolutionary biology is one of encoding without an encoder. According to this logic, complexity can indeed be produced according to a code constructed of simpler elements, but this fact does not require us to posit an author of those rules and hence a more complex entity at their origin (a positing that, as many, including Richard Dawkins, have noted, undermines theoretical explanation insofar as the answer is even more enigmatic than the enigma one sought to answer).

The idea of encoding predates, of course, the development of both cybernetic and genetic theories by centuries. The original meaning of code, or *codex* in Latin, was a series of laws, as in the code of Justinian or of Hammurabi, and the Latin word itself evolved from the earlier *caudex*, meaning trunk of a tree, from which the wooden tablets used for inscribing such codes were hewn. In a usage now obsolete, *code* also carried an explicitly religious connotation, as in the code of Christian and Jewish sacred writings that together made up the Christian scriptures. This seeming semantic heterogeneity belies a fundamental unity, however. Whether meaning law, foundational religious text, or system of rules underlying the construction of complex bodies or tasks, a code is primarily the symbolic simplification of some construct, process, set of actions, or experiences. Where the action or construct in question may be complex, sometimes dizzyingly so, the code for its construction is relatively simple. This simplicity allows for its recollection, transmission, and reproduction.

Perhaps the element of reproduction or repetition is of greatest importance here. In the seventeenth century, the originator of the idea of the modern cybernetic machine, Gottfried Leibniz, argued that there could be no such thing as true repetition. What became known as his principle of the identity of indiscernibles claimed that were two things to be alike in every possible way, they would not in fact be two things but one thing. For the philosopher Immanuel Kant, whose own thought was in many ways a response to the very differ-ent ideas of Leibniz and the English philosopher David Hume, this principle was the result of Leibniz's failure to distinguish between appearances, about which one can have knowledge, and how things are in themselves, about which one can have no knowledge.

If the principle of the identity of indiscernibles were valid, Kant said, it could be so only for a through-and-through intellectual world, one independent of the forms of intuition through which we come to know the world: space and time. Appearances, in contrast, which need space and time to be manifest, would need to be discernible from one another even while the identity of their referent remained the same. If this were not the case, to take an example from another story by Borges, the appearance of a dog seen from the front at 3:14 and the appearance of the same dog seen from the side at 3:15—which are two discernible appearances because they occur at different moments in time and in different spatial configurations—would have to refer to two nonidentical dogs. But for Kant, the appearances of the dog are both identical (it is the same dog) and yet discernible (we distinguish between them in space and time). We must, in other words, be capa-ble of discerning self-identical objects in space and time in order to perceive them as objects in the first place.

For Leibniz's "intellectualization of the world," then, the world or how we perceive it is identical to *the idea* of the world, or its code. For any self-identical entity there is a specific code, and the repetition of that code means the repetition of all its possible attributes and can result only in its perfect reproduction as a self-identical thing. The example to keep in mind here is of a digital versus an analog repro-duction, say a CD recording of a piece of music as opposed to a tape or vinyl recording. In theory, the music on a CD can be reproduced ad infinitum without suffering from generational decay, because what is being passed down is a series of information packets that are then read anew each time. The analog model of reproduction would be much more resonant with the world described by Kant, in that each new copy registers the fact that it is in a different space and time. Generational decay is due to the fact that the music here is not identical to its code but is embodied in a material format that regis-ters minute changes in time and space. The accumulation of such changes leads to greater and more noticeable changes at greater spatial and temporal remove.

In some respects, though, even the example of digital transmission does not resolve Leibniz's problem. Kant would merely point out that each time we play the CD constitutes a different temporal and spatial appearance of the music's code. The fact that we recognize and can say that the tune is identical each time we hear it depends entirely on there being a difference to begin with, a time between the hearings and another set of spatial coordinates across which we can recognize the identity of the tunes. Perhaps a more challenging example would be that of a hypothetical full immersion in a virtual reality, such as the one presented in *The Matrix*. There the protagonists' bodies, their motor-sensory apparatuses, are in one world while their senses are totally involved in a world produced by code. The appearances produced by the Matrix, one might conclude, are identical to their code. Each time an encoded sequence repeats, the same set of sensory output is produced—one series produces exactly this experience of red, another precisely this taste of a madeleine. Yet on closer analysis we see that exactly the same problem arises. The code may be the same, but the material embodiment of the code, how it is read or interpreted by the sensory apparatus, is necessarily discernible in time and space—if not, then were Proust in the Matrix he would not remember the taste of the madeleine as coming from his youth and hence yearn to regain that lost time.

Leibniz's theory is ultimately based on a conviction that the substance of the world is equivalent to its information, which is in part why he both engaged in the popular seventeenth-century project of the creation of perfect, rational language and experimented with some of the first prototypes of the modern computer, a machine that calculates by translating instructions written in a binary code. While the project to create a machine capable of calculating as well as the binary code that eventually enabled modern computing were real innovations, the search for the perfect language—and the conviction underlying it that the world could indeed be the expression of a single language or master code—is an old one, as I have just shown. By adopting it to his purposes, Leibniz essentially translated into a modern, scientific framework a set of religious and philosophical convictions dating from the earliest foundations of Western culture.

Nevertheless, while the ideology underlying and propagating the image of the world as code was often religious, it would be a mistake to believe that the resistance to this image emerged from a skepticism or denial of religious belief. As I have pointed out, the opposite is true: on the one hand, to the extent that our modern worldview has adopted an implicit belief in the code of codes, that belief has informed secular thought as easily as it informs religious thought; on the other hand, to the extent that a real possibility of resistance to the code of codes has developed, it has done so thanks largely to a tradition of skepticism *within* religious thought toward the idea that creation could ever be reduced to a kind of knowledge even in principle accessible to human beings.

Although both Leibniz and Kant were religious men, in the sense that their philosophies explicitly addressed the existence of God, in some way they each represent one possible path for a post-Enlightenment secular humanism. Which path one takes depends on which set of assumptions one adopts about the nature of the world and our knowledge of it. For those who take the Leibnizian approach, humans inhabit a world with their senses, to be sure, but everything we sense is reducible to a specific code, an underlying language that, when unlocked, will give us access to the universe. Once the code is broken, secrets as impenetrable as, for example, the consciousness of another human being will be open doors for us. Like the characters in a Philip K. Dick novel, we will be able to decide in the morning what mood we'll be in that day, and pain, sorrow, and anger will be feelings we can avoid by turning the right dial.

For a Leibnizian, furthermore, the cosmological structure of space-time is already there, lying in wait for us. While it's true that I cannot know what number my roulette ball will land on, the fact that *it will have landed on* a given number is an incontestable fact and one that will be revealed to me simply at the right time and place. Take the following example from the string theorist Brian Greene. Two friends sit in chairs separated by some 10 billion light years. The reality of each one consists of what he sees around him in his own vicinity. But to be perfectly fair, each would have to admit that whatever the other has around him is just as valid a reality as his own. The problem is, if one friend starts moving toward the other, his "now slice"—the slice of space-time containing everything that is occurring right now—suddenly adjusts to include events that, from the perspective of the other friend, *have not happened yet.* As Greene puts it of the two friends in his example, "something that seems completely undecided to us is something that, for him, has already happened . . . In this way of thinking, events, regardless of when they happen from any particular perspective, just *are.* They all exist. They eternally occupy their particular point in space-time."

Another version of this idea was popularized by the Harry Potter series. One of the brilliant magical devices imagined by its author J. K. Rowling is called a Pensieve, a sort of bowl into which wizards can deposit their memories. But unlike writing or recording or even a video camera, the Pensieve captures the past not from any particular perspective but as it in fact happened. In this way, when Harry puts his head into the Pensieve to experience someone else's memory, he is able to notice things outside that person's horizon of attention. In other words, the Pensieve makes present the whole slice of space-time around a person's memory and allows the viewer to explore that slice in ways the owner of that memory never did.

Both the string theorist and the children's author share a basic, Leibnizian assumption: the universe as it exists outside our perceptions or even our ability to perceive nonetheless exists *as if it were being perceived.* The world as it is in itself, in other words, already exists as knowledge. In the case of the Pensieve, what it has to capture is not a memory but the space-time of a memory in all its possible configurations, known from every angle, moving in every direction, at every possible speed and, to push the example to its extreme, known in every way possible: known by a seeing human, or by a bat using sonar, or by a blind hound dog relying on its sense of smell. Likewise, Greene's two friends, in order to experience now-slices that might include each other's future events, must be separated by a distance so great that only a God could, even in theory, compare those events and make judgments about our respective knowledge of them. Indeed, what would a knowledge that could encompass such distances even look like? As Greene himself points out elsewhere, it may well be that the nature of the observer is intrinsic to all observed identities and events, just as a piece of music requires an ear and a brain to synthesize the otherwise disparate vibrations of which it is composed, and a painting requires an eye and brain to join its disparate paint strokes into a unified picture.

In other words, while each of these examples depends on a perfectly commonplace image of how the world is in itself, there is no evidence whatsoever that the world is in fact like that. There is and can be no evidence that our future events already exist for the perspectives of distant observers. This is a fiction engendered by mathematical descriptions of space-time that are accurate for their own purposes but do not translate into the casual observation of friends and their surroundings. Likewise, Pensieves make for terrific devices in stories of magic, but we have no reason to believe that the past exists in any such objective way that would allow it to be explored like a virtual reality environment.

Skepticism toward such an objectifying view of space-time is what differentiates the Kantian from the Leibnizian path. For Kant, when we humans make observations of the world, we necessarily do so in time and space, but the fact that we do so tells us nothing about the world as it is independently of those observations. That is to say, from a Kantian perspective, the world may well be like the one Greene and Rowling speculate about, but it is in principle impossible for us to know that because knowing anything involves for us changes over time and space, and such changes over time and space are radically incompatible with knowing the world as it is independent of those changes. From a Kantian perspective, then, to decide that my future events are already part of another person's now-slice would make no more sense than deciding what a Chopin concerto sounds like outside of time or one of Monet's paintings outside of space. The very presupposition requires a kind of knowledge that is incompatible with perceiving the event, music, or painting in the first place.

As I said, both Leibniz and Kant allowed for religion in their thought. But as thinkers on the threshold of Enlightenment modernity, they were also paving the way for future thinkers who would do entirely without the notion of God or even actively militate against religion. In each of their systems, God had a specific role to play. For

Leibniz, God set the universe in motion and guaranteed through a pre-established harmony that the various elements of the universe, from atoms to souls, would give the appearance of interaction, even if none was really happening. Kant, in contrast, thought of God as a regulative ideal, a kind of necessary supplement to thought without which we would fail to arrive at truths about the world, and fail to govern our actions according to our duty. Aside from believing in God in this way, however, Kant insisted that we could no more know anything about God's will than we could know about the universe as it is itself, which, as I've suggested, constituted an inherent impossibility for him.

But by believing in God in this way and not believing that we could know his will, Kant argued that we accomplished something very important. A belief concerning ultimate metaphysical truths that was held strictly separate from our knowledge about the world would free us to pursue science unimpeded by fanaticism and dogma. Concomitantly, a belief in God that made no claims to being supported by demonstrable knowledge would allow for tolerance between faiths and eventual peace between nations. This is the ideal of religious toleration that made its way, albeit through different philosophers, into the U.S. Constitution, and it is this ideal that protects us from fundamentalisms of all kinds. It is the religious toleration that accompanies and stems from moderate religious belief and agnosticism about metaphysical matters, in other words, that best protects not only the rights of others to practice their own faiths and pursue their own version of happiness but also knowledge from the stagnation threatened by the code of codes.

How Religions Became Fundamentalist

A conclusion from what I have argued so far would seem to be that fundamentalist thinking, whether religious or otherwise, has always existed, even while it has been accompanied by ways of thinking that undermine it or criticize it from within. This conclusion, however, contradicts some recent work in the history of religions that suggests that fundamentalism, contrary to how it is often perceived in popular culture and the media, is a profoundly modern phenomenon. Karen Armstrong has made this argument by distinguishing between two kinds of knowledge, which she expresses with the Greek terms *mythos* and *logos*. Whereas mythos refers to a holistic knowledge that is metaphoric at heart, logos designates a focused, pragmatic kind of knowledge best exemplified by specific problem solving. Whereas mythos forms the basis of our cultures and their self-understandings, their sense of right and wrong, of what is heroic or abhorrent, what to be admired and what to be ashamed of, it makes no pretension of describing physical objects and their functioning. Logos, in contrast, is the kind of knowledge that tells us a lot about the physical world we inhabit; it comes from observation and experimentation and permits us to intervene in highly successful ways in our environments.

For Armstrong, both kinds of knowledge have their respective places in any society. A society that tries to solve practical problems through the application of mythos, however, is bound to run into serious problems. Likewise, the use of logos to regulate every aspect of human cultural, spiritual, or psychic life has the potential to do great harm. In this light, she goes on to claim, modernity can be seen in some ways as the ascendancy of logos over mythos; where Western and other cultures had traditionally valued both forms of knowledge—the creative, metaphoric, all-encompassing weltanschauung of mythos and the pragmatic, problem-oriented, representational thinking of logos—modernity and the success of the scientific revolution led to an almost total suppression of mythos from the realm of "serious" intellectual endeavor. Rather than valued as another realm and way of articulating beliefs, mythos came to signify a childlike and obsolete attempt to explain the world, an endeavor now pursued to far greater effect by the scientific method.

As the Western logocentric worldview grew in power and influence during the scientific revolution, areas of social and personal life that used to be approached under the aegis of mythos were dealt with as if they were objects to be manipulated. The assumption began to dominate intellectual circles that every aspect of existence, including cultural practices and human desires and beliefs, could be explained through objectively discoverable physical laws. While this assumption did indeed lead to some breakthroughs in medicine, psychology, and economics, it also produced its own excesses. As I point out in the next chapter, a society that denies that humans have a cultural and psychical existence that is not reducible to physical causes risks alienating aspects of existence that humans cling most desperately to. Arguably some of the worst political atrocities of the last century, specifically those stemming from certain interpretations of Marxist "scientific materialism," were direct results of this kind of thinking.

The other effect of an excess of logocentric thinking has to do with what happens to the sorts of beliefs usually contained in mythos when mythos is denied as a valid category of experience. This, according to Armstrong, is the origin of the specifically modern phenomenon of religious fundamentalism. Faced with a uniformly logocentric standard for truth claims, defenders of religious faith begin to interpret religious texts and teachings in a way that had never been normal practice before, namely, *literally*. Already in the seventeenth century Sir Isaac Newton, perhaps the greatest scientific mind before Einstein but also a religious fanatic, had become obsessed with purging Christianity of mythical doctrines. Since Newton could understand doctrines like that of the Holy Trinity only in literal terms, he could make no sense whatsoever of them, unlike the earlier Gregory of Nyssa, who found in the Trinity an image he could use to express "the unnameable and unspeakable."

Such a backlash, in fact, is at the origin of the term *fundamental ism*, which was coined by U.S. Protestants in the early years of the twentieth century as a rallying call against mainstream theological tendencies such as the so-called higher criticism, which had been emphasizing a return to more nuanced and metaphorical interpretations of the liturgies since the late nineteenth century. Already in the 1880s, Dwight Moody had founded the Moody Bible Institute in Chicago in an effort to defend against the higher criticism. And between 1910 and 1915, the oil millionaires Lyman and Milton Stewart funded the publication of twelve paperbacks called *The Fundamentals*, which sold some 3 million copies. Fundamentalism was born.

Whether Christian or of other faiths, the movements we call religious fundamentalism are always the result of a perceived attack on a given community of faith. This is one reason why the attempt to regulate or restrict religious practice, what the new atheists are in essence calling for, has always resulted in and can only result in more fervently held beliefs, often in the form of fundamentalist backlash. In other words, when secularists criticize all religion, the unintended consequence of their actions is strengthening exactly that aspect of religious belief and practice that is ultimately at odds with modern, democratic values.

This dynamic can be seen in Europe today as modern, secular states like France grapple with the Islamic practice of veiling women. Far from successfully inculcating a sense of equality between men and women of all faiths, attempts to restrict public demonstrations of religious affiliation like the veil have led to backlashes, such that many women who wear it today in Western countries like France are doing so as a sign of cultural identity and anticolonial sentiment. Likewise, we tend to view the famous Scopes "Monkey Trial," which was eternalized in the 1955 play and 1960 film *Inherit the Wind*, as having revealed the depths of belief in creation science already present in fundamentalist communities. But as Armstrong has argued, before the Scopes trial few fundamentalists actually believed in creation science or thought it particularly important to do so. Creation science became a hot-button item for the fundamentalist movement only after William Jennings Bryan's defeat in court by Clarence Darrow was ridiculed by the journalist and essayist H. L Mencken, who wrote in an obituary for Bryan that he "lived too long, and descended too deeply into the mud, to be taken seriously hereafter by fully literate men, even of the kind who write school-books." In the face of such humiliating condescension, groups tend to close ranks around tenets and practices that define them as different from the outside world.

Similar stories abound in the history of the current Islamic fundamentalist movements. I should point out, however, that the term *fundamentalist* is very contested as regards scholarship on contemporary Islam. It has been translated into Arabic as *usuliyyah*, which refers to the study of sources, a practice that, as most scholars would be quick to note, is not of particular importance to the people we refer to as fundamentalists. Instead of as "fundamentalist," scholars of Islam have tended to designate these movements as "radical," "extremist," or "puritan." Regardless of the name, the same phenomenon alluded to in discussing Christian fundamentalism can be seen at work in the recent history of Islam. As with the Christian case, Islamic fundamentalist movements have emerged largely as a backlash against enforced modernization and perceived humiliation, with the added aspect of violent political repression not present in the Christian case.

Many scholars point to Sayyid Qutb as one of the principal figures of present-day radical Islam. Qutb traveled and studied in the United States for several years before returning to his home country of Egypt and joining the Muslim Brotherhood. Both Qutb and the brotherhood became more radical in response to direct oppression from Nasser's regime, a shift echoing that of Islamist movements in other parts of the Middle East, most notably in Turkey, Iran, Algeria, and Syria. As Bernard Lewis has documented, an uprising on the part of the Muslim Brothers in the city of Hamāh in 1982 was put down by the Syrian government at a cost of somewhere between ten thousand and twenty-five thousand lives. And in 1992, the Algerian military staged a coup with the support of the French government and most of the Western world in order to overthrow the newly elected Islamic FIS and throw its leadership in jail, giving Muslims of the world another example of the Western double standard regarding democracy and self-determination. It is cases such as these that have led Lewis to argue that Arab terrorism has its origins and causes really in nationalist sentiment and desire for self-determination, not in any religious doctrine.

For Karen Armstrong, the fundamentalist backlash in religions since the dawn of modernity has constituted a kind of perversion of the original essence of these faiths. She claims that most if not all the faiths that are widely practiced today originated in what she calls, following Karl Jaspers, the axial age, the time between more or less 900 and 200 B.C.E. when the major tenets of all the world's principal systems of thought emerged, albeit in different parts of the world. She includes in this list Confucianism and Taoism in China; Hinduism, Buddhism, and Jainism in India; monotheism in Israel; and philosophical rationalism in Greece. Many of the ethical insights of these different traditions are the same. They all, for example, produced some version of the golden rule, which was designed to eradicate the egotism that had brought societies at the time into crisis and which is still at the heart of just about every religious and ethical system in existence today. In their religious manifestation, axial faiths therefore all require kenosis, or the self-emptying essential to some theological interpretations of Christian love. Another axial principle is that of the ultimate transcendence of the universe, whether conceived of in material or spiritual terms. In other words, the axial traditions agreed that, however we conceive of the world, no human can ever be understood as having the last word; knowledge is an infinite process. At their core, then, the world's religions were never about doctrine or the literal interpretation of the divine will but about generosity and tolerance for others. When they have degenerated into dogma, they have betrayed that original purpose.

As religions have developed and evolved they have also stagnated and grown sedimented layers of dogma. In the face of social conflict they have become fortresses of group identity and been deployed to measure purity of commitment and foster intolerance for others. But despite these changes religions carry with them the core of their original purpose. I have mentioned how the Judaic and Christian theological traditions emphasize the ineffability of God's ultimate knowledge, but the Koran too insists that God communicates through symbols because thought cannot contain him, and no revelation can be definitive. Furthermore, the Koran also holds other faiths to be authentic, and Muhammad told his followers to pray toward Jerusalem because the God they prayed to was also the Jewish and Christian God.

Since the attacks on the United States of 9/11 there has been no shortage of speculation about whether Islam has a special relationship to intolerance and violence. Shortly after the attacks UCLA scholar of Islamic Law Khaled Abou El Fadl published an essay titled "The Place of Tolerance in Islam," in which he claims that while Islamic history has shown a tendency for extremist groups to be ejected from mainstream Islam, just as they are in other religions, Islam today is living through "a major shift, unlike any it has experiences in the past." While Islamic thought traditionally "tolerated and even celebrated divergent opinions and schools of thought," the "institutions that once sustained and propagated Islamic orthodoxy—and marginalized Islamic extremism—have been dismantled." In the absence of these mainstream institutions—which Abou El Fadl claims is due to state interference in religious matters in the Muslim world—Islamic puritans have had a platform from which to proclaim themselves the true representatives of the Muslim faith. Under their tutelage, Abou El Fadl goes on to argue, passages from the Koran that seem to support intolerance and Muslim supremacy have been read out of context and emphasized, while other passages insisting on religious tolerance and the ineffability of God's will have been ignored. In particular, Abou El Fadl quotes the Koran 5:49, which reads: "To each of you God has prescribed a Law and a Way. If God would have willed, He would have made you a single people. But God's purpose is to test you in what he has given each of you, so strive in pursuit of virtue, and know that you will all return to God, and He will resolve all the matters in which you disagree."

A commentator on Abou El Fadl's text, Mount Holyoke professor of international studies Sohail Hashmi, argues that while premodern Islamic societies and, indeed, the Koran itself were both accommodating of diversity and recognized the complexities and ambiguities of faith, more Islamic commentary and scholarship has been guilty of occluding this tolerant legacy with its interpretations and even translations of the sacred text. In another response, *New Left Review* editor Tariq Ali echoes Bernard Lewis's contention that, ultimately, violent or intolerant tendencies in present-day Islam have little to do with theology and everything to do with political realities. Whether the Koran or the New and Old Testaments, sacred texts have as many possible interpretations as they do readers; what really matters is political oppression, poverty, and the feeling of being disrespected or degraded.

As mentioned, popular culture and the media tend to think of religious fundamentalism as a kind of embarrassing leftover from a less-informed, less-educated past. As Nicholas Kristof, a columnist whom I deeply admire, wrote in a recent column about the increase of troops in Afghanistan, "It breaks my heart that we don't invest in schools as much as medieval, misogynist extremists." I certainly understand Kristof's point, but while the Taliban are indeed misogynist extremists, there is nothing medieval about them. Prior to the onset of modernity in the sixteenth century, and especially prior to the expulsion of the Jews and later the Moors from Christian Spain, European thought benefited immeasurably from the intermingling of Islamic, Jewish, and Christian intellectual and theological traditions. While religious intolerance was no doubt also an issue during the Middle Ages, it is a gross mistake to associate religious fundamentalism with bygone times.

Although I agree with Karen Armstrong that modernity's dismissal of mythos as a legitimate form of knowledge is the underlying factor for religious fundamentalism today, I'd like to pinpoint more specifically why that is the case. At the core of all fundamentalist thought is the belief that the world exists as a kind of knowledge, that it can be known as it is in itself if only we learn to read the code. While this belief has existed in many cultures at many times, one of the functions of the axial religions was to undermine that conviction, to teach people that the transcendent nature of ultimate reality was such that no human could ever, in principle, come to know the ultimate truth. What is crucial to grasp is that this core principle simultaneously sustains the existence of mythos and logos as two separate but equal domains of knowledge; for if the ultimate, all-encompassing questions are by nature infinite, if human knowledge in principle cannot grasp everything, then practical, objectifying logos is simply not relevant to such discussions, and the holistic, metaphoric standards of mythos have their place. Likewise, to the extent that modernity has allowed mythos to be pushed aside by the practical successes of the scientific method, the axial principle of the transcendence of ultimate knowledge has been weakened. But it is this principle that more than any other works to defend humanity from the dangers of its own certainty. It is for this reason that modernity's privileging of logos over mythos, in Armstrong's terminology, has paved the road for a specifically religious fundamentalism, namely, by weakening that aspect of religious traditions that has been the most effective critical weapon they have against the fundamentalist impulse: moderate belief.

4 Faith in Science

Partial Truths

On May 6, 2007, at the first Republican debate of the 2008 presidential race, the Republican presidential hopefuls were all asked to raise their hand if they did not believe in the theory of evolution. Senator Sam Brownback, Congressman Tom Tancredo, and Governor Mike Huckabee, three important members of the legislative and executive branches of government, all raised their hands. A few days later, in light of the outsized reaction to a moment in the debate that lasted only a few seconds, Sam Brownback published a clarification in the form of an op-ed piece in the *New York Times*. In that piece he sounded a moderate tone, claiming that what he opposed was not evolution per se but the extrapolation from evolutionary theory that mankind was necessarily an accidental development. Seeking to occupy a reasonable middle ground, he argued that science and faith should not be opposed to each other but should respect each other's contributions to human knowledge:

> Biologists will have their debates about man's origins, but people of faith can also bring a great deal to the table. For this reason, I oppose the exclusion of either faith or reason from the

discussion. An attempt by either to seek a monopoly on these questions would be wrong-headed. As science continues to explore the details of man's origin, faith can do its part as well.

While there is no surprise in a politician's wishing to come down firmly on both sides of an important issue, Senator Brownback's apparent moderation dissimulates an ulterior motive. As he puts it in the last lines of his piece: "While no stone should be left unturned in seeking to discover the nature of man's origins, we can say with conviction that we know with certainty at least part of the outcome. Man was not an accident and reflects an image and likeness unique in the created order." Science is fine, in other words, as long as it is used to confirm what we already know about mankind's place in the world.

This is the main problem with most attempts to strike a moderate tone by reconciling faith and science. By assuming that religion can sit at the same table with scientific knowledge and make contributions to its goals, those who strive for a consensus between the two ultimately create an implicit and necessary hierarchy in which one side works to confirm a view of the world that the other already knows. And it is not just religious believers paying lip service to science who repeat this error; very often the scientists who have come out in favor of reconciling faith and reason have taken this same path. A truly moderate religious position, however, rejects this kind of reconciliation. The faith of religious moderation does not foster science because the two are compatible, but because they are radically *incompatible*. To agree with the late evolutionary biologist Steven Jay Gould, faith and science are nonoverlapping magisteria; both have a place in our lives not because they are both concerned with the same ultimate goal but because they are concerned with two essential aspects of human existence that are radically, necessarily different from each other. Or, to put it another way, faith and reason are compatible not because religious tenets are in themselves reasonable but because it is eminently reasonable that humans hold profoundly important beliefs that are not grounded in reason or dependent on evidence. Evidence-based reason is one, very important kind of belief, but there is no evidence-based argument for holding that it is or should be the only kind of belief.

Francis Collins, the geneticist whose book I discuss in the previous chapter, sounds the same note in various ways in the course of his defense of his own religious belief. In the context of his slow conversion from atheist to Christian, he says the following:

> It also became clear to me that science, despite its unquestioned powers in unraveling the mysteries of the natural world, would get me no further in resolving the question of God. If God exists, then He must be outside the natural world, and therefore the tools of science are not the right ones to learn about Him. Instead, as I was beginning to understand from looking into my own heart, the evidence of God's existence would have to come from other directions, and the ultimate decision would be based on faith, not proof. Still beset by roiling uncertainties of what path I had started down, I had to admit that I had reached the threshold of accepting the possibility of a spiritual worldview, including the existence of God.

The idea that God must be outside the natural world may not strike all readers as particularly intuitive. While some Christians might have a vague idea of the kingdom of God as being not of this world, others will recall Luke 20, in which Jesus responds to the Pharisees' question about the coming of the kingdom by telling them, "The kingdom of God does not come with your careful observation, nor will people say, 'Here it is,' or 'There it is,' because the kingdom of God is within you." Nonbelievers, in turn, might pointedly wonder what it means for God to be "outside" the natural world, whether that means he is therefore not present at all in the natural world, and where this other, nonnatural world must therefore be.

Nevertheless, Collins's claim has a well-established philosophical and theological history. In fact, a philosopher he repeatedly refers to in his book is one of the key figures of the Enlightenment, the German thinker Immanuel Kant. I go into a bit more detail later in this chapter about Kant's essential insight and what it means for religious moderation, but first let's take a brief look at what Kant meant by insisting on a strict separation of the natural world from God, since this is also the basis of Collins's reasoning.

According to Kant, all the knowledge we have of the world comes through our senses. Our senses, in turn, tell us about the appearances of things, and these appearances come to us over time, either changing or remaining the same, and through space, showing us some aspect of things and not others. Kant's main philosophical argument was about the importance of not forgetting this limitation: no matter what we claim to know, we really only ever know the world as it appears to us over time and through space. Once we accept that limitation, however, we are tempted by the possibility of another kind of knowledge, one that could know the world not merely as it appears to be but as it really is, in itself. Kant called this knowledge noumenal and insisted that, properly used, noumenal ideas could be used only as limit concepts, that is, used to remind us of what we cannot know. The noumenal would be, properly speaking, the realm of God: the ultimate reference point for a kind of knowledge we cannot possibly have.

I think Collins is right on track when he uses Kant to mark a strict separation between the world of science and the world of beliefs. The problem arises when he and other believers themselves inadvertently fail to respect this divide. A now classic theological temptation comes in the field of cosmology. Given the near consensus on the origin of the universe some 13.7 billion years ago in an event called the Big Bang, metaphysical speculation naturally emerges as to what, if anything, came before the Big Bang. Collins is no exception, and though cosmology is not his field, he enthusiastically cites the astrophysicist Robert Jastrow, who sees in the Big Bang a kind of mirror story to the one told in Genesis: "Now we see how the astronomical evidence leads to a biblical view of the origin of the world. The details differ, but the essential elements and the astronomical and biblical accounts of Genesis are the same; the chain of events leading to man commence suddenly and sharply at a definite moment in time, in a flash of light and energy." As Collins goes on to say: "I have to agree. The Big Bang cries out for a divine explanation. It forces the conclusion that nature had a defined beginning. I cannot see how nature could have created itself. Only a supernatural force that is outside of space and time could have done that."

These are the sorts of statements that create big theological and philosophical problems for believers, in precisely the same way that statements about the impossibility or extreme improbability of God's existence create problems for nonbelievers. When Collins enthuses that the Big Bang cries out for a divine explanation and that nature could not have created itself, he forgets the strict limitations he had earlier placed on human knowledge and strays into the realm of what Kant called fanaticism. Accepting a divine explanation for the Big Bang is tantamount to shutting down scientific inquiry, which has certainly not forgone its theoretical endeavors in the face of the daunting physical conditions present at the beginning of time. In fact, this is precisely what the fields of string theory and multiverse theory are all about. And as Brian Greene has strenuously argued, string theory is not nonfalsifiable, because the mathematical models it proposes for the beginning of time have potentially observable consequences for the visible universe that emerged from the Big Bang. As for the claim that nature could not have created itself, there are some theories in the field of supersymmetry that claim just the opposite, namely, that absolute nothingness would be so unstable that existence itself could indeed spontaneously generate!

Another recent book written in a similar vein to Collins's volume is Joan Roughgarden's *Evolution and Christian Faith*. Like Collins, Roughgarden is both a scientist and a practicing Christian. And like Collins, she sees no incompatibility between her scientific and her religious beliefs. Unlike Collins, though, Roughgarden does not even pay lip service to the kind of Kantian separation between faith and science that I am defending here. In fact, her stated goal is diametrically opposed to this position. As she expresses it in the opening chapter of her book,

> What evolutionary biologists are finding through their research and thinking actually promotes a Christian view of nature and of our human place in it. Thus, as Christians we don't have to simply stand aside and say, Well, science is about the material world and religion about the spiritual, and ne'er the twain shall meet. Instead, we can rejoice as Christians in the ethical meaning behind what evolutionary biologists are increasingly finding.

As she forecasts, Roughgarden then goes on to read passages from the Bible alongside facts drawn from evolutionary biology in order to show that there is no contradiction between the two.

After a brief discussion of the core finding of evolutionary biology that all life is related, Roughgarden quotes a series of passages from Genesis and concludes, as she has promised, that there is no conflict there. Her failure to come up with conflicting claims leads her to wonder "why the impression is widespread that evolutionary biology somehow conflicts with the Bible." And as she goes on to write, "I've scoured the Bible for text relevant to the finding that all of life belongs to a common family tree, but can't find passages pertaining directly to the particular fact." Not wishing to be curmudgeonly, I nonetheless find it hard to believe that this argument can seriously be offered as defending the proximity of evolution and Christian faith. I could just as well claim that the total absence of any mention of bacterial flagella in the Bible is adequate evidence for believing that Christianity is *in*compatible with evolutionary biology. It seems fair to claim that no nonbeliever would take this argument seriously. While there may be nothing in the Bible denying the interconnectedness of life, there is plenty of language in favor of, well, just take your pick: the creation of the cosmos in seven days, the creation of mankind prior to other animal life, God's creating Eve out of Adam's rib because Adam was feeling lonely, the list goes on.

Despite their good intentions, scientists who look for evidence for religious belief in the natural world are doing damage to their own cause. By accepting that faith is on the same plane with scientific knowledge and is concerned with the same questions, they implicitly or explicitly concede that the beliefs people of faith claim to hold should be held to the same standards of evidence as those of scientific knowledge. But if they are, they will not last long. The moment we treat religious articles of faith as descriptions of the natural world, we begin to treat God as a hypothesis, just as Dawkins says we should. And when that happens, I see no other conclusion for any reasonable person to draw than the one Dawkins predicts and advocates: the existence of God is very, very improbable.

On the other hand, there is no reason that the scientists who happen to be believers need make the mistake of keeping their belief systems on the same plane. Owen Gingerich, formerly a professor of astronomy and the history of science at Harvard University, has eloquently defended his Christian belief as being utterly nonconsequential in terms of his scientific practice. As he explains, "Choosing to believe that the universe was designed makes no difference to how a scientist practices science, it is a metaphysical choice." Note that Gingerich specifically refers to the notion of the universe as having a design. In his book *God's Universe*, Gingerich advances a notion of design that is a counterexample to the idea defended by intelligent design theorists. Whereas the latter claim that the theory of natural selection fails to explain the observed evidence and that the assumption of a divine creator does a better job, Gingerich's idea of cosmic design does not compete on any level with existing or potential scientific descriptions of the universe.

The difference between the two notions of design depends on the Aristotelian distinction between efficient and teleological causes. For Gingerich, science is concerned with the former—what specifically causes this or that phenomenon—whereas religion is concerned with the latter—what the ultimate purpose of existence is. Intelligent design theorists confuse the two sorts of design by inserting divine intervention within an efficient causal chain; for instance, since the bombardier beetle's ability to blast superheated fluid from its abdomen could not have evolved by chance, it must reflect the intervention of a divine creator. In contrast, Gingerich's notion of design is teleological and could never be used to explain any given phenomenon and hence block a scientific inquiry into its efficient cause. The teleological cause Gingerich believes in is life; in other words, he believes the ultimate purpose of the universe is to make life possible. Whether you accept or reject this belief is, as he has put it, inconsequential to how you are going to conduct your science; it is a metaphysical interpretation of the evidence.

The evidence in this case refers to the so-called initial settings argument. According to current cosmological theory, the relative stability of the universe appears to be far from assured. On the contrary, the basic mathematical parameters of the widely accepted inflationary model of the Big Bang must be "fine-tuned" to an extraordinarily small range in order to explain how the observable universe could have come into existence at all. Similarly, the existence of carbon-based life forms like us requires a seemingly incongruous stability in the carbon nucleus making it surprisingly unlike other heavy elements. These special qualities in the carbon atom were predicted by the great Cambridge astronomer Fred Hoyle and later demonstrated by the American astrophysicist Willie Fowler, earning him a Nobel Prize.

These fine-tuning arguments have often been countered by the so-called anthropic principle, which I have heard evoked in a tongue-in-cheek way as the blade of grass in a fairway that, when hit by a golf ball, screams, "What are the chances!" In cosmological terms, the anthropic principle states merely that we shouldn't be surprised by any degree of improbability we discover in the initial settings of the universe since we would be even more unlikely to discover the settings of a universe that could not produce us. Regardless, the crucial point is that, unlike intelligent design theorists, Gingerich represents the example of a scientist whose religious belief remains strictly separate from his scientific practice. And while the difference with Francis Collins is more subtle, it is still vital: where Collins and Jastrow apparently believe that the Big Bang proves the existence of a creator, Gingerich modestly, and moderately, chooses to interpret the fine-tuning of initial settings as an indication of cosmic design and purpose.

Keeping articles of faith and descriptions of nature on two separate planes is a good idea not merely because it makes strategic sense for people of faith; it's a good idea because faith of a moderate kind serves as a constant reminder to science not to overextend its reach, not to make assumptions about our knowledge of the world that cannot be demonstrated through any possible form of observation. Atheist critics are right when they point to religious fundamentalism as justifying horrific atrocities in the name of God's will. But they are necessarily silent when equally horrific atrocities have been committed in the name of such pseudoscientific ideas as historical necessity, scientific materialism, or racial purity. But the fault is of the same kind. What Kant called fanaticism and I am calling fundamentalism takes hold when believers of any stripe think they have access to a knowledge without limits, when they think they hold the copyright on certainty. The unifying condition of all moderate faith is the knowledge that no one will ever have the final answers. This knowledge fosters tolerance in matters religious and curiosity in matters scientific because just as it undermines any religious doctrine that claims to trump all others, it also reassures us of the never-ending nature of our quest to understand the world we live in.

Why Freedom Has Nothing to Fear from Darwin—or from God

In an influential article in the *Annual Review of Neuroscience*, Joshua Gold, of the University of Pennsylvania, and Michael Shadlen, of the University of Washington, sum up the state of the art in experiments over recent decades aimed at discovering the neural basis of decision making. At first glance these studies would appear to put a final nail in the coffin of human freedom. In one set of experiments, researchers attached sensors to the parts of monkeys' brains responsible for visual pattern recognition. The monkeys were then taught to respond to a cue by choosing to look at one of two patterns. Computers reading the sensors were able to register the decision a fraction of a second before the monkeys' eyes turned to the pattern. Since the monkeys were not deliberating but rather reacting to visual stimuli, researchers were able plausibly to claim that the computer could successfully predict the monkeys' reaction. In other words, the computer was reading the monkeys' minds and knew before they did what their decision would be.

The implications are immediate. If researchers can in theory predict what human beings will decide before they themselves know it, what is left of the notion of human freedom? How can we say that humans are free in any meaningful way if their decisions can be known by others before they themselves make them? Research of this sort can seem frightening for many reasons. This is probably because an experiment demonstrating the illusory nature of human freedom would, in many people's minds, rob the test subjects of something essential to their humanity.

But what are we presuming about human beings that makes these results so potentially dangerous? Clearly there is a political calculation involved. No one who has lived in the twentieth century, from Orwell's dystopian visions of totalitarian states to the brainwashing fears of the Korean War, can fail to see how the image of researchers predicting human decisions would present a threat to American ideals. But if we delve a little deeper, what is it, precisely, about predictability that poses such a threat to freedom?

Many scientists and specifically brain researchers might be forgiven for responding that an unacknowledged religious bias lies at the heart of such fear. Their argument certainly has merit. If a well-positioned machine can tell me what I am about to decide before I decide it, this means that, in some sense, the decision was already taken before I became consciously involved. But if that is the case, then how am I, as a moral agent, to be held accountable for my actions? If, on the cusp of an important moral decision, I now know that my decision was already taken at the moment I thought myself to be deciding, does this not undermine my responsibility for that choice? And if a consciously deciding agent is the model in many religions for the soul, doesn't the agent's lack of moral responsibility ultimately deprive the soul of what is most essential to it? For without freedom of choice, a soul becomes merely a cog in the machine of nature, its actions and choices predetermined, the morality and ultimately the very meaning of its existence left in tatters.

For their part, theologians have also spent a great deal of time ruminating on the problem of determination. The Catholic response to the theological problem of theodicy—that is, of how to explain the existence of evil in a world ruled by a benevolent and omnipotent God—was to teach that God created humans with free will. It is only because evil does exist that humans can be free to choose between good and evil, and hence that the choice for good has meaning. As the theologians at the Council of Trent in the sixteenth century declared, freedom of will is essential for Christian faith, and it is anathema to believe otherwise. Protestant theologians such as Luther and Calvin, to whom the Trent statement was responding, had disputed this notion on the basis of God's omniscience. If God's ability to know were truly limitless, then his knowledge of the future would be as clear and perfect as his knowledge of the present and of the past. If that were the case, though, then God would already know what each and every one of has done, is doing, and will do at every moment in our lives. But how can I truly be free if God already knows how I am going to choose in every instance I am faced with a decision? According to the theology of predestination, I can't. Predestination holds that my freedom is an illusion; that who will be saved and who will be damned has been decided since the beginning of time, and there is nothing my individual choices can do to change that fact. And as to why, given such a reality, I should choose to behave well and follow the laws of God and my community, well, that's really only a question of saving appearances. If I behave well then the chances are that I am one of the saved, which makes me feel good about myself and look good in the eyes of my neighbors as well.

So it appears that, even if the source of resistance to a deterministic model of human behavior is religious, a religious perspective can still lead one to a deterministic position. In fact, when religion and science square off around human freedom, the irony is that it is human freedom itself that gets lost; science and religion often end up on remarkably similar ground. The reason for this is that both science and religion are basing their assumptions on an identical understanding of what the world and our knowledge of the world are like. In this view, human freedom is a kind of straw man from the get-go, because the entire world and everything in it, including a human brain and the decisions it makes, are conceived of as existing on a spatiotemporal continuum that takes the form of something intrinsically knowable, either by God or ourselves. In other words, whether human behavior is "determined" by God or nature, the implicit model we are using assumes that being determined means already existing in a knowable form.

Let me explain what I mean by way of an example. Imagine we suspend a steel ball from a magnet directly above a vertical steel plate, such that when I turn off the magnet, the ball hits the edge of the plate and either falls to one side or the other. Now we adjust the position of the magnet so that when the ball hits the plate, it falls more or less half the time on one side and half the time on the other. Given this setup, it is virtually impossible to measure the myriad conditions affecting the ball's trajectory with the accuracy necessary to predict the ball's trajectory. We can guess, but the success rate of our guesses will converge on 50 percent the longer we extend the experiment.

Now, I assume that very few people, having accepted the premises of this experiment, would conclude from its outcome that the ball in question was exhibiting free will. Whether the ball falls on one side or the other of the steel plate, we can all comfortably agree, is completely determined by the physical forces acting on the ball, which are simply too complex and minute for us to monitor. And yet we have no problem assuming the opposite to be true of the application of the monkey experiment to theoretical humans: because their actions are predictable they can be assumed to lack free will! In other words, we have no reason to assume that either predictability or lack of predictability has anything to say about free will. The fact that we do make this association has more to do with the model of the world that we subtly import into such thought experiments than with the experiments themselves.

Predictability of decisions can be associated with a lack of free will only if we assume two things: first, that the faculty for making decisions is somehow not located in the physical structures of the brain; and second, that the origin of the decision somehow existed prior to its prediction as well as prior to the subject's conscious apprehension of it. The first assumption is the one we normally associate with religious belief, and yet mainstream religious practitioners of all stripes have demonstrated complete comfort with the idea that their own religious experiences takes place in the brain and can be mapped using current imaging technologies. Andrew Newberg has done precisely such experiments with Buddhist monks and Christian nuns, creating brain scans of experts in meditation and prayer prior to and during their activities, and none of his subjects has been even slightly disturbed to learn that their ecstatic states or even feelings of encountering God can be mapped on a brain scan. In other words, the attribution of a nonphysical seat for decision making, a ghost in the machine or disembodied soul, is simply not a requirement of religious thought or of a philosophical account of free will. It is, however, a straw-man version of free will, since it is precisely such an image of freedom that would be undermined by experiments predicting human decisions.

The second assumption is even more profound and goes to the heart of the argument I've been making throughout this book. This assumption, which I have termed the code of codes, holds that the universe exists in space and time as a kind of knowledge waiting to be discovered. As I discussed in the previous chapter, this image of the universe has a philosophical and religious provenance and has made its way into secular beliefs and practices as well, but it is also the necessary ingredient in fundamentalisms of all kinds. In the case of human freedom, the code of codes works by convincing us that a prediction somehow decodes or deciphers a future that already exists in a coded form. So, for example, when the computers read the signals coming from the monkeys' brains and make a prediction, belief in the code of codes influences how we interpret that event. Instead of interpreting the prediction as what it is, a statement about the neural process leading to the monkeys' actions, we extrapolate about a supposed future as if it were already written down and all we were doing was reading it.

Imagine the monkey experiment again, but now we replace the monkeys with human subjects. We ask those human subjects to look at a series of choices—left, right, up, down—and then to move their eyes in the direction of their choices. As with the monkeys, our computers successfully "predict" the human subjects' choices. In each case, the computer registers which direction their eyes will move a fraction of a second before their eyes in fact move, and we can keep a record of that time lag as proof that free will is a myth. But is that really what we have proven?

If we think carefully about it, we can readily see that such an experiment will have failed to rule out not only free will but even the decision-making influence of a soul! It is well established that neurons allow charges to travel through the brain at speeds well below those achieved by electrical signals traveling through metal circuitry. If a disembodied soul did guide our actions from its seat in, say, the pineal gland (as Descartes surmised), the activation of certain neurons in the brain could easily be read by sensors faster than they could achieve their desired outcome in the human body.

In other words, all that such experiments demonstrate is that decisions are embodied affairs, and that embodied affairs take time, neither of which is a threat even to religious notions of free will, much less to a philosophically and scientifically adequate notion of free will. But what would this latter notion look like? What kind of freedom is compatible with a scientific, mechanistic understanding of the human brain, without imposing on science the unscientific (because nonfalsifiable) idea of an immortal soul or ghost in the machine?

The philosopher who probably gave the most complete answer to this question was Immanuel Kant. In Kant's view, the main mistake philosophers before him had made when considering how humans could have accurate knowledge of the world was to forget the profound and necessary difference between our knowledge and what we have knowledge of. At first glance, this may not seem like a very easy thing to forget; after all, anyone who thinks about it at any length will probably come to the conclusion that, for example, what our eyes can tell us about a rainbow and what a rainbow is in itself must be pretty different things! But Kant argued that our failure to grasp this difference was more far-reaching and had greater consequences than anyone could have thought.

Taking again the example of the rainbow, Kant would argue that while most people would grant the difference between the range of colors our eyes perceive and the mist refracting the light that causes this optical phenomenon, they would still maintain that more careful observation could indeed bring one to know the rainbow as it is in itself, apart from its sensible manifestation. This commonplace understanding, he argued, was at the root of our tendency to fall profoundly into error, not only about the nature of the world but also about what we were justified in believing about ourselves, God, and our duty to others.

The problem was that while our senses can bring us verifiable knowledge about how the world appears to them only in time and space, our reason always strives to know more than appearances can show it. This tendency of reason to always want to know more is and was a good thing. It is why humankind is always curious, always progressing on to greater and greater knowledge and accomplishments. But if not tempered by a respect for its limits and an understanding of its innate tendencies to overreach, reason can lead us into error and fanaticism.

Here is how Kant argued this would work: faced with the uncertainty of how the world might be in itself when not encountered by a being like us—a being who has to encounter things in an extended way over space and sequentially over time—reason would naturally reconstruct that unknowable world in terms it could understand, namely, in spatial and temporal terms. In other words, when asked to describe realities that transcend the limits of a knowing subject situated in a particular place at a given time, realities such as the universe in its totality, the origin of space and time, or the identity of God, reason would drop all caution and have at it, translating those realities into the very spatial and temporal forms that they transcend.

As this may still sound somewhat abstract, let's return to the example of the experiment predicting the monkeys' decisions. What the experiment tells us is nothing other than that the monkeys' decision-making process moves through the brain, and that our technology allows us to get a reading of that activity faster than the monkeys' brain can put it into action. From that relatively simple outcome, we can now see what an unjustified series of rather major conundrums we had drawn. And the reason we drew them was because we unquestioningly translated something unknowable—the stretch of time including the future of the monkeys' as yet undecided and unperformed actions—into a neat time line. We treated the future as if it had already happened and hence as a series of events that could be read and narrated.

From a Kantian perspective, with this simple act we allowed reason to override its boundaries, and as a result we fell into error. The error we fell into was, specifically, to believe that our empirical exploration of the world and of the human brain could ever eradicate human freedom or, for that matter, interfere with matters of faith. Freedom, for Kant, is equivalent to the radical incompatibility between human knowledge and the world as it is in itself. Freedom is not and can never be at risk because, try as we may, we cannot close that gap; we may convince ourselves that with our science we can achieve a knowledge of the world in itself, but we are in error in thinking so. Because we necessarily know things from a moment in time and from a place in space, even the postulate of a "God's-eye view" that would, from a Protestant theological perspective, condemn us to a predestined damnation or redemption is ultimately as irrelevant to our real freedom as the myriad earthly forces that undoubtedly do determine our physical existence. As much as we owe the nature of our current existence to the evolutionary forces Darwin first discovered, or to the cultures we grow up in, or to the chemical states affecting our brain processes at this very moment, none of this impacts on our freedom. I am free not because a ghost inhabits the machinery of my brain or because that machinery cannot yet be adequately mapped; rather, I am free because neither science nor religion can ever tell me, with certainty, what my future will be and what I should do about it. I am not free because I can make choices but because I must make them, all the time, even when I think I have no choice to make.

Far from undermining human freedom or even the rationality of religious belief and practice, current work in cognitive science and neurology is finding itself more and more in agreement with moderate theology. In his thoroughgoing evisceration of the "new atheists," theologian John F. Haught correctly notes that Harris, Dawkins, and Hitchens never bother to submit their own assumptions to the test they propose for religious belief, namely, that one should accept no belief without evidence. For what evidence can they possibly offer, he asks, that this very postulate is correct, that all knowledge worth knowing can be verified by evidence? Indeed, present-day brain research demonstrates that there is very little scientific basis for arguing that human knowledge can ever be based entirely on reason, much less on a strictly evidentiary, objectivist understanding of the world.

Let's take the case of memory. As anyone can quickly grasp, the most perfectly reasoning mind would be utterly useless without some kind of memory. Even short-term calculations depend on the retention of the values to be calculated, and any serious reasoning requires an enormous amount of content to be brought to the table, for which both short- and long-term memories are indispensable.

But if the first thing any serious brain researcher will tell you about memory is how extremely fallible it is, then the second will be how utterly dependent the brain is on emotions when deciding what memories to emphasize and thus retain. As Hopkins neuroscientist David Linden has put it,

> We need a signal to say, "This is an important memory. Write this down and underline it." That signal is emotion. When you have feelings of fear or joy or love or anger or sadness, these mark your experiences as being particularly meaningful. These are the memories you most need to store and keep safe. These

are the ones that are most likely to be relevant in future situations. These are the building blocks that form logic, reasoning, social recognition, and decision making.

Emotions underlie logic and reasoning, and emotions, as most people will recognize, are very often beyond our conscious control. We feel joy, love, anger, and sadness when situations befall us, when we encounter people whom we are attracted to or are special to us, or when our values are violated, or when we lose what is dear to us. Thus reason, to which the atheist critics would like us to hold all our judgments, rests precariously on a highly individual latticework of emotions, contexts, and values.

The extraordinary complexity of this latticework poses a challenge to our self-understanding. We strive and often may make serious progress in comprehending our own emotional lives, but our ability to articulate this complexity is limited both by the potentially infinite nature of what we are trying to comprehend and by the limited tools at our disposal.

Neuroscientists distinguish between declarative and nondeclarative memories. Unlike nondeclarative memories, which are triggered by stimuli in the local environment, declarative memories are consciously recalled. But while they are for that reason more under our conscious control, they are also, as Linden explains, "embedded in a much richer informational system." In other words, the memories we consciously call to mind in order to tell a story, explain something about ourselves, or figure out a problem are invariably dependent on a deeper, richer store of nondeclarative memories, themselves stored in a variety of areas in the brain.

Linden has argued that one of the neurological explanations for what he calls the religious impulse is that "our brains have become particularly adapted to creating coherent, gap-free stories and that this propensity for narrative creation is part of what predisposes humans to religious thought." But far from using this insight to deflate religious belief, Linden finds no incompatibility between faith and science. As he makes clear (and I couldn't agree more!), "It's only *fundamentalist* religious thought that is incompatible with science." The reason Linden's scientific explanation for why humans have a propensity for religious belief doesn't undermine religious belief is because Linden, like moderate believers, understands how very porous our knowledge of the world is. "Science," as he says, "*cannot prove or disprove* the central ideas underlying most religious thought." By most religious thought, however, he means what I have been calling moderate belief, belief that does not make claims about measurable appearances in the world. What fundamentalists and some atheists share, in contrast, is the assumption that science can prove or disprove those ideas. The difference is that fundamentalists believe in only those "scientific" findings that are compatible with their beliefs, and atheists believe that the discoveries of science definitively disprove all religious beliefs.

When Linden argues that the brain is predisposed to religious belief, he locates this tendency in what we could call its narrative faculty, that is, humans' ability to create coherent stories about their past, their identity, and the world around them. The content of these stories are, of course, declarative memories, which, as mentioned, themselves rest on a latticework of unconscious, nondeclarative memories. It turns out that this narrative faculty is specific to one of the brain's two hemispheres, and it is not surprisingly the one that also houses our linguistic abilities.

Some fascinating experiments with patients whose cerebral hemispheres have been separated in an effort to control their severe epilepsy have shown to what extent the left brain is engaged in creating coherence out of incoherence. In such "split-brain" patients, each hemisphere still functions normally; they just do not communicate with each other. When the patients are shown two screens, with each screen visible to only one eye, the hemispheres can be exposed to different images such that the right hemisphere doesn't see what the left one sees and vice versa. In one experiment, a patient's left hemisphere (through his right eye) was shown a chicken claw, and his right hemisphere (through his left eye) a snowy landscape. The patient was then asked to use each hand to choose a card from a selection lying in front of him. The right hand (controlled by the left hemisphere) chose a chicken, and the left hand (controlled by the right hemisphere) chose a shovel. Each of these choices reflected a direct association, of course. The trouble was that, as the two hemispheres were not communicating, neither one was aware of what the other had seen. When the patient was then asked why he had chosen a shovel along with the chicken, he quickly explained that the shovel was used to clean out the chicken shed.

Linden interprets this as evidence that, given an otherwise inexplicable scenario, the left brain (which is responsible for conscious communication and hence is the side answering the question) will create coherence and believe in it. The left brain, to put in another way, suffers a kind of intolerance for incoherence, leading Linden to theorize that "the left cortex's always-on narrative-constructing function promotes the acquisition of religious thought through both subconscious and conscious means." This conclusion conforms to the findings of other neuroscientists, such as V. S. Ramachandran of the University of California, San Diego, whom Linden quotes as follows:

> The left hemisphere's job is to create a belief system or model and to fold new experiences into that belief system. If confronted with some new information that doesn't fit the model, it relies on Freudian defense mechanisms to deny, repress or confabulate—anything to preserve the status quo. The right hemisphere's strategy, on the other hand, is to play "Devil's Advocate," to question the status quo and look for global inconsistencies.

So, if the left hemisphere suffers from a kind of incoherence intolerance, the right hemisphere appears to have no such qualms and to be, in fact, quite open to incoherence. The right hemisphere, however, is also responsible for those very emotions that so powerfully underlie our ability to remember certain facts and events and that, as Andrew Newberg has argued, bestow on our beliefs their sense of reality.

Newberg's work is so important to understanding religious belief because he has created neural images of religious practitioners of various faiths and even atheists while meditating or praying as well as while not doing so. His findings are remarkable: no matter what the religious affiliation or lack thereof, the meditators were able to decrease the activity of an area in the brain called the parietal lobe, which is responsible for our sense of orientation in space and time. In other words, whether through prayer, thinking of God, or through other forms of meditation that focus on an image or on bodily awareness, practitioners are able to reduce the activity in that area of the brain that is in part responsible for locating our selves and hence are able to lose themselves in prayer or meditation. It is also not surprising that these practices should be accompanied by increased activity in some of the key areas in the right hemisphere and depression of activity in the left sphere, for heightened awareness of context at the expense of a coherence of self is one of the principal reported effects of both meditation and prayer.

The point I am making in citing these recent findings in neuroscience is, first, that there is no scientific evidence whatsoever for atheist claims that reason is or even can be the principal much less the exclusive guide to human judgment and behavior. Second and perhaps even more important, however, this research suggests that the formation of our beliefs is the result of a delicate interaction between the brain's regions and hemispheres and that the ways we believe may depend on the relative contribution of those different regions. For example, while the emotional investment in a fundamentalist belief system certainly comes from the right hemisphere, the intolerance of incoherence that is the hallmark of fundamentalism and essential to the formation of any kind of overarching interpretation is a left-hemisphere function. It is very likely, in other words, that an intolerance of incoherence combined with a fierce emotional attachment can develop in human subjects regardless of whether they embrace a religious belief system or some other kind. Alternatively, there is much evidence to suggest that some religious and spiritual practices such as prayer and meditation are particularly adept at priming the right brain's function of accepting incoherence and finding emotional stimulation in a loss of self and of one's tight, coherent worldview. Such practices, it stands to reason, would be inimical to fundamentalist tendencies.

Finally, there has been research suggesting that while believers may be more gullible and susceptible to error than skeptics, they are also more creative and open to new ideas. Again, I find this unlikely to be true of fundamentalist believers, who are by definition less likely to be open to anything crossing their own belief system; so the default position is that these believers are what I am calling moderates. In a series of experiments carried out by neurologists in Zurich, believers were more likely than skeptics to find words and patterns in randomly scrambled letters. Skeptics, on the other hand, were more likely not to see words that actually were there. These differences were correlated with higher dopamine levels in the brains of believers, which researchers suggested might be a prerequisite for creativity.

Such findings corroborate my sense that moderate religious belief—belief, in other words, that depends on a tolerance for inconsistency and incoherence, belief in things that cannot be proven or disproven rather than belief against evidence—is perfectly compatible with and perhaps even helpful in the progress of human knowledge. If we cease to think of science as a purely passive endeavor, a kind of mental photography of a world waiting for us to break its code and reveal its secrets, and instead understand it as what it in fact is, a thoroughly human and spectacularly creative process, then an individual's ability to engage in multiple forms of belief can be seen as supportive of the scientific endeavor rather than in competition with it. Poetry, and specifically metaphor, the ability to take one thing for another, has been theorized by some philosophers as perhaps the most powerful force in human thought. Rather than passively picturing the world as it is, we humans use our inherent metaphoric capabilities to create a participatory knowledge that constantly imagines what is not the case and what could be the case in addition to what is de facto the case. In this view, literal representations of the world, far from being the basis of all thought, are merely one piece of the puzzle and are inconceivable outside a larger and far more complex process of engagement. Nonliteral interactions with the world, including moderate religious belief, literature, philosophy, painting, are themselves indispensable to thought; the arts and humanities, culture and religion, are thus not just pretty window dressings that we can get to when we can afford them while math and science are hard-core truths. They are all core activities of human creativity, of which the scientific endeavor is just one focused aspect.

Unintelligible Design

Since I am a scholar of literature, it's often not obvious to people I talk to why I am writing a book about religion. When I am asked, I usually tell them that the path to writing this book led through my reading, teaching about, and writing about the work of the great Argentine poet and author Jorge Luis Borges. One short story by Borges, which I have read and talked about in seminars countless times, has perhaps more than any other single source caused me to reflect on the issues in this book.

In 1941 Borges published his short story "Tlön, Uqbar, Orbis Tertius," about a secret society that set itself the task of creating a world in exhaustive detail. According to its creators, the people of that world, the planet of Tlön, had invented an idealism so systematic, so realistic, that the mere imagination of something to be found usurped the resistance of reality, and that thing would emerge in the real world as it had been imagined. In a postscript to the story that Borges postdated to 1947, six years and a world war away from his own moment in time, he writes eerily, enigmatically of the incursion of Tlön into the real world:

> Almost immediately reality gave way in more than one regard. The truth was it desired to give way. Ten years ago whatever symmetry with the appearance of order—dialectic materialism, anti-Semitism, Nazism—was enough to bewitch men. How not to submit to Tlön, to the minute and vast evidence of an ordered world? It is useless to reply that reality is also ordered. Perhaps it is, but in accordance with divine laws—I translate: inhuman laws—that we will never perceive. Tlön may be a labyrinth, but it is a labyrinth woven by men, a labyrinth destined to be deciphered by men.
>
> The contact with and habits of Tlön have disintegrated this world. Enchanted by its rigor, humanity forgets and forgets again that it is a rigor of chess masters, not of angels.

According to the story, Tlön was originally the creation of a secret society of natural philosophers dating to the seventeenth century whose ambition was to create a country in all possible detail. When the project emigrates to the United States sometime around 1824, one of its American inheritors, a certain Ezra Buckley, "speaks about it with some disdain—and laughs at the project's modesty. He says that in America it's absurd to invent a country and instead proposes the invention of a planet." In the story, the character Borges (Borges often included himself as a character in his fictional pieces) first learns about Tlön's existence through an oblique reference made over dinner by his friend and sometime collaborator Adolfo Bioy Casares to "one of the heretics of Uqbar," who had declared that "copulation and mirrors are abominable, because they multiply the number of men."

To Borges's protestations of incredulity, Bioy swears he read about the country of Uqbar in the 1917 edition of *The Anglo-American Cyclopedia*, "a literal, but also morose, reprint of the *Encyclopaedia Britannica* of 1902." Some on-the-spot research leads to no results, but Bioy later produces the copy in question, in which some four pages appear in the elsewhere nonexistent space between the entry for Uppsala and the end of volume 26—a volume, Borges notes with a tinge of resigned annoyance, whose spine incorrectly indicates its range as falling between *Tor* and *Ups.*

Uqbar is, as it turns out, the tip of an iceberg, a trace of that initial project to create a country that later metastasized into the international transgenerational society of Orbis Tertius, whose purpose is the creation of Tlön, a world contained in an encyclopedia. Borges's rediscovery of Tlön opens a Pandora's box of sorts, as Tlön's own philosophical investment in the exclusive existence of ideas and the illusory nature of material reality ends up invading and permeating our own world, the world of Borges the narrator and his readers. The prophetic nature of the postscript is strangely disguised by its author's pretending to have penned it long after the time he actually did; nevertheless, it reads with a somewhat postapocalyptic tone. Its author speaks to us from a time when it is apparently too late to avoid the catastrophe we should have seen coming.

And what is the catastrophe? Just as the power of the idea, of the word, holds sway over material reality in Tlön, so too does the mere idea of a perfectly organized world hold sway over the imagination of men. The problem, Borges says, is our inability to distinguish properly between a rigor of chess masters and a rigor of angels. We invent worlds, invent systems, and then see in those aspects of the world that are not of our invention the traces of the same organizing rigor we have put into our inventions; in confusing the rigor of chess masters with a rigor of angels, we confuse the order of our ideas with the order of being. When we do so, our fictions have a strange tendency to become reality.

For me this story has been a powerful catalyst for thinking about the dangers of certainty. In Borges's poetic expression, the certainty underlying fundamentalisms of all stripes is a matter of humanity's repeated failure to distinguish between a rigor of angels and one of chess masters. As he writes in that haunting postscript, the mistake we are always tempted to make is to assume that the order we in fact observe in nature means that nature is ordered according to our kinds of laws. When Borges writes that if reality is ordered it is ordered according to divine laws, he immediately translates this to mean inhuman laws. In other words, what Borges is theorizing in this brilliant, prophetic story is the very nature of fundamentalist thinking that I have been calling the code of codes. When he admonishes us that the laws that order reality are divine only insofar as they are not perceivable by us, this is another way of saying that the way the world is in itself is not a kind of knowledge, and no one will ever have direct access to it. This is not to say that we cannot and should not seek to understand reality, to describe it to the best of our abilities and refine those descriptions ever more. But the danger he identifies emerges when we fail to understand that these descriptions and attempts to understand are always our own and never can or will correspond to how reality is independently of our descriptions of it.

The final prophetic aspect of Borges's story concerns the nature of the danger itself. If the cause is the failure to respect the difference between our knowledge of reality and how reality is in itself, the danger this failure produces is the effect on how we perceive reality. In Borges's story, this is represented by the incursion into lived reality of imaginary objects, a kind of blurring of the boundaries between reality and fiction. But isn't the worldview of most fundamentalists also a kind of imposition on reality of a certain fantasy scenario? In the case of religious fundamentalists this is particularly clear given that for those of us not sharing their belief system the contention that they know with certainty the world was created six thousand years ago or that they will be rewarded in heaven for blowing themselves up is no more reasonable than believing that Spiderman or Harry Potter or

Luke Skywalker are real people who really can spin webs, use magic, or control the force. But nonreligious fundamentalisms distort reality as well, if perhaps in more subtle ways. In each of the cases I discuss in chapter 2, for instance, the assumption that beliefs are grounded in certainty led people to different judgments, different behaviors, and different ways of treating other people than would have otherwise been the case.

While I've already pointed out that religious moderation undermines all rationale behind believing in intelligent design, in truth its criticism goes even further. From the position of religious moderation, what's really impossible is *intelligible* design. While intelligent design is a bit of a straw man at this point, it is far more difficult to see how assumptions concerning the intelligibility of nature's design are also fundamentalist at the core. Indeed, many defenders of science who (rightfully) mock intelligent design theorists for their presumption of a purposeful, intelligent designer don't hesitate to assume that whatever design the universe has is through and through intelligible, that is, understandable as it is in itself without any limits or restrictions.

In the spring of 1991, New York–based literary agent, author, and intellectual impresario John Brockman published a manifesto in which he forcefully argued that the public exchange of ideas had been for too long dominated by what he called the literary intellectuals. These intellectuals, he charged, were involved primarily in "metacommentary," that is, rather than injecting their own ideas or discoveries into the public sphere they tended to make arguments on the basis of other people's ideas and discoveries. In place of these figures, Brockman proposed to use his considerable clout to usher in an "emergent third culture" made of hard scientists who not only were themselves at the forefront of knowledge but also could write eloquently about their own insights and innovations. Once the educated public was exposed to Brockman's circle of scientists and "digerati," so the reasoning went, literary intellectuals and cultural theorists would lose their influence. Instead of sappy speculation we would have cold, hard truth served to us with verve and biting wit by the members of Brockman's "reality club."

The verdict in Brockman's manifesto is merciless. In his piece he quotes American writer Stewart Brand as saying,

Science is the only news. When you scan through a newspaper or magazine, all the human interest stuff is the same old he-said-she-said, the politics and economics, the same sorry cyclic drama, the fashions, a pathetic illusion of newness and even the technology is predictable if you know the science. Human nature hasn't changed much; science does, and the change accrues, altering the world irreversibly.

While Brockman excludes the arts from Brand's opprobrium, he shifts the blame onto the literary intellectual. "The Reality Club is filled with artists," he points out. "And the artists are almost like a weather vane for society, they have their antenna out checking these new ideas and filtering them through their work rendering them visible in different ways and feeding them back. But I haven't seen the same from the literary intellectual crowd."

True to his word, Brockman has become the puppet master in a concerted and largely successful effort to populate (and dominate) the public discourse with scientist-writers. His elite client list includes Murray Gell-Mann, Richard Dawkins, Daniel Dennett, Paul Davies, Nicholas Humphreys, Steven Pinker, and many other noted scientists and proscience philosophers. Together these brilliant thinkers have largely succeeded in marginalizing the more cultural and literary-minded intellectuals and contributing to the broad perception of the literary intellectual as a washed-up remnant of knee-jerk sixties radicalism holed up in an Ivy League bastion reciting strange and incomprehensible slogans about deconstruction and signification that make sense to no one, including himself.

It may well be that Brockman was right to fire off his broadside in 1991. Many today would agree that literary theory had become too insular and self-absorbed while simultaneously claiming to have an entitled opinion about everything. But the intellectual culture Brockman has established in this country has been dominant for two decades, and as with most dominant parties, it too has taken things too far. When C. P. Snow coined the term "third culture" at the end of the 1950s, what he had in mind was a dialogue between scientists and humanists, not a full-fledged takeover of the public debate by one of those parties. The dismissal of the humanist as having nothing of importance to say about "reality" has had, to my mind, a specific and detrimental consequence: it has led to the fomentation of a kind of science fundamentalism among the educated elite of this country that puts them at odds with a broad cross section of the American public in a way that may be counterproductive to the promotion of science and scientific reasoning.

One of my favorites of Brockman's posse, and indeed an extremely influential voice for the educated public today, is Harvard professor of psychology Steven Pinker. Pinker has been an outspoken critic of what he has called in a subtitle to one of his recent books "the modern denial of human nature." According to Pinker, recent academic culture has become enamored of the idea that the human being is born a blank slate, a purely malleable creature that cultures, languages, and political forces mold into its adult form. As he puts it in the introduction to that book,

> When it comes to explaining human thought and behavior, the possibility that heredity plays any role at all still has the power to shock. To acknowledge human nature, many think, is to endorse racism, sexism, war, greed, genocide, nihilism, reactionary politics, and neglect of children and the disadvantaged. Any claim that the mind has an innate organization strikes people not as a hypothesis that might be incorrect but as a thought it is immoral to think.

My first response upon reading these words was that Pinker is exaggerating both the prevalence and the rhetorical excess of the tendency we could generally describe as social constructivism. While there is no doubt that certain academic fields such as anthropology, sociology, and literary theory emphasize cultural and social forces in their analyses of human behavior, this would seem to follow from the fact that these fields are concerned with, well, culture and society. Implicit and explicit claims that social and cultural forces have dominant responsibility for shaping human behavior must certainly be taken in that context and could hardly be that widespread.

Nonetheless, Pinker does document statements regarding the origin of behavior that are truly jaw-dropping, including claims "that little boys quarrel and fight because they are encouraged to do so; that children enjoy sweets because their parents use them as a reward for eating vegetables; that teenagers get the idea to compete in looks and fashion from spelling bees and academic prizes; and that men think the goal of sex is orgasm because of the way they were socialized." If nothing else, Pinker's talent for collecting droll examples of academic eccentricity leads to enjoyable reading; but his claim, of course, is weightier by far.

To Pinker's eye, such far-reaching claims have infiltrated the culture at large and led to undesirable social consequences. One example he cites is the pressure parents feel to produce picture-perfect children. Indeed, if we are all truly convinced that nurture rules and that nature is a kind of passive backdrop to be overcome by techniques and devices from gender-neutral child rearing to Baby Mozart, when our children fail to grow into models of social justice or Rhodes scholars, we parents have to shoulder the guilt for our failure.

This sounds very reasonable. But pause for a moment to consider the problem if the poles were reversed. What if we imagine the case of brilliant, highly successful parents producing children who uniformly fail to rise to their hopes and expectations, or of a hopeful single mother who selects a sperm donor on the basis of his high IQ only to find that her child develops a merely mediocre intellect. Can there be any doubt that such relative failures would also provoke disappointment and self-doubt? While it's probably the case that such an occurrence, although doubtless quite normal, could inspire less anguish and soul-searching, this has less to do with popular assumptions about human nature than with a pragmatic recognition that it's a lot harder to change our genes than our child-rearing techniques. In that way most people are probably living implicitly according to the words of Reinhold Niebuhr's serenity prayer, accepting the things they cannot change and hoping to change the things that they can.

The point in both of these examples is not, then, merely that we are wrong to pin it all on nature or nurture; I would guess that most people have come to the reasonable conclusion by now that we are all made up of some mixture of the two. Rather, what is at stake is the implicit assumption that human beings and their behavior are things that could in principle be mapped out and understood with such precision that they could ever be perfectly predicted and controlled.

Later in his book Pinker expertly explodes the dilemma at the heart of the ageless debate between freedom and determination by pointing out that even probabilistic indeterminacy as regards behavior (the idea that a murderer had, say, a 99 percent chance of killing his victim as opposed to a 100 percent chance) does not return the responsibility of a free will to the subject in question. "In fact," he goes on to say,

> there is *no* probability value that, by itself, ushers responsibility back in. One can always think that there is a 50 percent chance some molecules in Raskolnikov's brain went thisaway, compelling him to commit the murder, and a 50 percent chance they went thataway, compelling him not to. We still have nothing like free will, and no concept of responsibility that promises to reduce harmful acts.

This failure of the concept of free will to ensure responsibility stems, as he notes, from the tendency, long ago noted by the English philosopher David Hume, to think of freedom in terms of physical causality, in which case, "either our actions are determined, in which case we are not responsible for them, or they are the result of random events, in which case we are not responsible for them."

Pinker's purpose in presenting this scenario and favorably citing Hume's pithy judgment on moral responsibility is to shift the question of morality away from whether or not we have it to why we have the concept in the first place. We can, he argues, both productively explain behavior and have a useful concept of responsibility as long as we keep in mind what purpose we want that concept to serve, namely, the deterrence of wrongdoing. But while I could not agree more that pragmatic notions of responsibility may still function in the face of better and better scientific explanations of our behavior (or, for that matter, of how environment and social upbringing affect our behavior), I see in Pinker's reasoning a powerful set of unexamined assumptions regarding not responsibility but explanation itself, regardless of whether the explanation is of a biological, psychological, or sociocultural nature. The mistake, in other words, does not lie in thinking that there could be a probability value in determining Raskolnikov's behavior that could guarantee his responsibility; it lies in thinking that we could ever successfully and thoroughly explain the social and biological complex we are calling Raskolnikov.

To be perfectly clear, I am not arguing that this minimal obscurity of Raskolnikov's being is because he has a soul that is forever free and undetermined; the free and undetermined soul is a religious interpretation of this essential limitation in human knowledge that keeps us from ever successfully objectifying our fellow humans. The unexamined assumption that it is possible for human knowledge to bridge this divide is not only responsible for the apparently irresolvable dilemma of freedom and determination but also at the heart of the current devaluation of the humanistic fields, which are dedicated to cataloguing, analyzing, and even enjoying the apparently infinite creative capacity of the human in the face of this unbridgeable divide. The dream of what the philosopher Daniel Dennett has called heterophenomenology—the ability, assumedly to be achieved by neuroscience at some future date, to experience another person's first-person experiences from the outside—is not merely technically unfeasible but in principle impossible. This is so because every human institution and form of interaction, from art and literature to politics and law and love and desire, depends on the ultimate opacity of other people's consciousnesses. The external inhabitation of another human's consciousness, in other words, is conceptually impossible in the same way as would be the perfect dryness of water: its fulfillment contradicts the very phenomenon it is seeking to explain.

This unexamined assumption, what we could call science's primary code of codes, can have the added unintended consequence of undermining the accuracy of the conclusions scientists draw from their own research. Long before he wrote his defense of human nature, Pinker used his training in linguistics along with his remarkable argumentative skills to eviscerate the theory of the anthropologist Edward Sapir and his student, linguist Benjamin Lee Whorf, that human thought is influenced by the languages we speak. Aside from pointing out basic mistakes in Whorf's reasoning as well as exaggerations in his factual claims—including one concerning the number of words Eskimos have for snow, which, Pinker notes, even when counted generously are not that many more than the English language can boast—Pinker's arguments depend on his rigid distinction between thoughts and words.

In his now familiar style, Pinker begins this argument by documenting or perhaps overstating the "conventional absurdity" of equating thoughts and words, and then goes on to ridicule it ad nauseam until finally coming to rest on the perfect truism that "if there can be two thoughts corresponding to one word, thoughts cannot be words." Since, he goes on to reason, thoughts and words are fundamentally different, when we speak a language we are essentially translating our thoughts from a single, universal "mentalese" into whatever language we happen to have learned. And since, finally, our natural languages are therefore nothing but differently learned ways of expressing one mental language, obviously claims that our natural languages (like our cultures or our upbringings) profoundly color the way we think or perceive reality are gross exaggerations.

Unfortunately, this argument is a perfect case of Pinker's assumptions regarding the ultimate intelligibility of human nature getting the better of his scientific precision. While it is likely that Whorf's linguistic relativism took the claim of the cultural determination of perception too far, more recent work in cognitive linguistics has turned out to support the idea that what language one speaks can indeed have measurable influences on perception. Furthermore, the notion of mentalese, while grounding Pinker's commitment at a linguistic level to a stable human nature that can, in theory, be completely mapped and explained, risks blinding us to the actual power of language and culture to influence how people think while adding nothing to our understanding of how actual languages are in fact structured. Pinker answers his own question about how thoughts can be words if we can have two thoughts for the same word when he points out, with regard to the extraordinary flexibility of our phonetic systems, that "actual sounds are different in different contexts." In an analogous way, different thoughts can correspond to the same word because words mean different things in different contexts.

This point is not as trivial as it may appear at first glance. Pinker and other Chomskyans make a lot of hay of the almost infinitely creative potential of the generative grammar, pointing out how even infants in the first stages of learning how to speak are using language creatively and perhaps even creating expressions never heard before. Such creativity, they argue, demonstrates that languages are not learned by mere repetition and that the human being must therefore have an innate language instinct, or mentalese. But this wonder at the novelty of how we use language may, in fact, be something like Leibniz's astonishment that no two leaves in the garden are alike, or the commonplace remark that no two snowflakes are the same; in other words, the novelty of language use stems in large part from the fact that every time we say a word we say it in a slightly or even very different context. In fact, what makes words useful at all is that they transcend and even connect different moments in time or places in space. In this light, the fact that we almost always are saying something new has nothing to do with the universal nature of a hidden language we are translating into English or French but with the marvelous nature of language that it can refer to something other than itself.

This is not to say that humans don't have a language instinct; in a very obvious sense the mere fact that humans demonstrably use language already proves that. And certainly there are commonalities as well as differences among languages, and searching for those commonalities and theorizing their common structure is a worthwhile endeavor. But Pinker overreaches in both his linguistic theory and his overall defense of human nature because he is enthralled by the promise of the code of codes underlying not only all languages but all of human behavior as well. Such a code, though, is strictly impossible. Not, again, because I am embracing some notion of an eternal and ineffable soul, but because the code depends on an ideal of perfect or ultimate intelligibility that is at odds with knowledge itself.

Since I began this section with a story by Borges, let me end with another one, one that shows better than anything else I can think of exactly what I mean by the impossibility of a perfect knowledge. When Borges's character Ireneo Funes falls off his horse and hits his head, he loses his ability to forget. From that moment on, Funes remembers not only every object he has ever seen but also every aspect of every object and every moment of his seeing of that object. The perfection of Funes's memory, though, soon becomes an overwhelming impediment. He is unable to assimilate new experiences; as Borges writes, he can perfectly recount the memory of an entire day, but it takes him an entire day to do so. He is surprised at his own reflection in the mirror every morning since his perfect memory records every minute difference that time imposes on him; and he becomes increasingly annoyed at the generality of language, that we should use the same drab word *dog* to refer to the animal facing one direction at 3:14 and another direction at 3:15.

The point of Borges's hilarious thought experiment is that, as he himself puts it toward the end of the story, no matter how many languages Funes learns it is hard to say that he is capable of thought. In attaining a perfect memory, Borges's character also inevitably loses the ability to think, because thinking necessarily involves generalization, abstraction, and the forgetting of minor differences. In truth, Funes could never be surprised at his own reflection, or annoyed at the generality of our use of language; for in order to feel either surprised or annoyed, he would have had to perceive the connection between those different moments in time and hence forget the difference between them, if only long enough to see that they were two distinct moments. At the most basic level, then, the sensual perception we depend on for any thought, any knowledge whatsoever, is itself produced through a complex process of remembering and forgetting, of immersion and abstraction that is inimical to the notion of knowledge as perfectible.

The story is thus the ideal thought experiment for considering what a God's-eye view would be like if there really were such a thing, and how the very idea of such a knowledge is in fact antithetical to the conditions under which we come to know something. By definition an absolute being, God could not partake in anything so partial as human thought, for which distinctions in time and space are essential. The impossibility of anything resembling a knowledge that God could have of the world thus puts the lie to the fundamentalist logic of code, and frees us for a different—and better—way of thinking about science and faith.

5 In Defense of Religious Moderation

The Real Divide

One of the most mordantly funny political cartoons I ever saw appeared shortly after 9/11. Above a caption reading "Moderate Taliban," a turbaned teacher instructs his eager students to fly airplanes only *half* filled with fuel into *medium*-sized buildings. If I had to laugh despite the horror that had inspired the cartoonist, it was because of the brilliance with which he had mocked the very idea of a moderate fundamentalist: oxymoronic to the extreme, the one term totally negates the other.

Yet it is precisely this oxymoron that atheists would have you believe best represents the truth when they write, as Sam Harris does, that the moderately religious aid and abet religious fundamentalism by raising their children as Christians, Muslims, or Jews. Atheists have to make this claim because the entire weight of their arguments rests on demonstrating the absurdity of taking scripture literally—the only problem being that a great cross section of their supposed target would do nothing other than nod their heads and laugh with them were it not for the fact that they, to their great surprise, are included in the group to be thus lampooned. The charge is based entirely on a presumptive guilt by association: by definition religious moderates do not take scripture literally, and hence the atheist's derision of what they believe simply has nothing to do with them. Moreover, religious moderates reveal in their practice another, very rational belief, one that atheists and fundamentalists alike appear not to be aware of: it is perfectly reasonable to distinguish in our lives between things about which we can have definite knowledge and those things in which we can only believe, and hope our beliefs guide us in the best direction. This belief—that there are very different kinds of belief and that some do not respond to the strict standards of reason—is far more reasonable than the irrational and ultimately false belief that all belief must be securely grounded in reason.

Atheists not only are on weak footing philosophically but they're getting their facts wrong as well. The evidence from recent surveys undermines both the claim that the United States is in the midst of a religious revival and, what's more important, the assumption that believers in the United States are mostly biblical literalists. In general, the percentage of people claiming adherence to a given religion has been falling in the recent decades, not increasing. Of those who do identify as adherents to a specific faith, fewer are Christians, and even fewer are Evangelicals. Given a range of five choices—religious, somewhat religious, somewhat secular, secular, and confused—only 37 percent of all adults chose "religious"; but when you limit the selection to adults under thirty-four years old, the proportion drops to 27 percent. Only 24 percent of those who are affiliated think their own religion is the only way to salvation, and fully a quarter of people who are believers regularly attend services outside their chosen religion; the presumption that belief is necessarily exclusive is thus not supported.

When Alan Wolfe's research group the Middle Class Morality Project conducted in-depth interviews with focus groups in a variety of communities around the country, they discovered that the vast majority were what Wolfe calls quiet believers, a category corresponding to what I am calling religious moderation. These believers are certainly committed to their faith, but they interpret that commitment in very different ways from how a fundamentalist would. For one thing, moderates reject that believing in their faith means that other people's faiths are therefore wrong. In the words of one of Wolfe's interview subjects, a Mormon and, as Wolfe describes her, a strong believer, "I don't feel good about one church coming out and saying, 'You're all wrong, and you're all bad,' I don't believe in telling everyone else that they're wrong."

Such explicit tolerance is the norm for religious moderates and, as Wolfe has demonstrated, is also the norm for a vast majority of Americans who nonetheless self-identify in surveys as believers. Obviously this kind of nuance is hard to see at first glance, because it requires probing into what people mean when they say they believe something. But it is clear that what they cannot mean is anything like a literal belief in the words of any sacred text. Indeed, among younger Evangelicals, less than half claim to believe that the Bible is the literal word of God, and among Catholics the number falls to 23 percent. American believers, it seems, are far more sophisticated than their atheist critics give them credit for.

Their sophistication, as well as their tolerance, is not alien to the theological history I traced in the third chapter. Indeed, while most moderate believers are unlikely to have studied Isidore or Maimonides, the idea that God's will is ultimately inaccessible to human believers arises again and again in their discussions of their faith. In his interview with Joyce Umber, a Baptist from Broken Arrow, Oklahoma, Wolfe noted that aspect of her quiet faith: it rejects religious absolutism as "presuming too much, not only about others, and not only about ourselves, but about God." In other words, tolerance in this case stems from religious belief and is not in opposition to it.

Wolfe sums up quiet belief in these terms:

[Quiet believers] do not believe in absolutes but in balancing what is right with what is practical. They distrust extremes, even those views they consider correct but that are asserted with too much finality. And they feel that one has to do one's best to understand, even when one does not agree with, those who think otherwise. Quiet faith, in their opinion, does not make headlines or win medals. It tends to get drowned out by the brash blaring of the media; the self-interest of groups and organizations, the certainties of ideologists, the indifference of social scientists, and, when it comes to religion in particular, the rantings of fanatics.

What a different view we are given of American religion when, instead of relying on the rhetorical flair of a few well-spoken pundits who base their accusations on cant and hearsay, we ask someone who has actually studied Americans and their beliefs. Of course we have a skewed view of what Americans believe; the extremes are louder than the quiet middle and sell more books to boot. One of the strikes against me as I tried to sell this very book was that a book about moderation wouldn't sell. When it comes to markets, whether something is true or not is apparently beside the point.

Two Ways of Being Religious

That events and things exist in the past, present, and future and that the world is ultimately knowable as it is in itself would seem to be fairly uncontroversial beliefs. They come across as rational and even commonsensical and not at all as the stuff of superstition and religion. And yet these beliefs are the heart of what we tend to think of as the most religious kind of thinking: fundamentalism. The reason for this is that fundamentalist belief depends on the believer's knowing, without any doubt, that there is a way to know things as they are, not just as they appear.

But this belief is not at the heart of all religious belief. Just as there are plenty of people who assume a fundamentalist attitude about the world without thinking they are religious, there are many people who are religious without assuming such an attitude at all. The openly Christian philosopher Gianni Vattimo, for example, has written that "when we recite the Credo, we use a number of purely metaphorical, allegorical expressions . . . A great many things in the Credo can't be taken literally." Or, as the evolutionary biologist Steven Peck, who is a practicing Mormon, expressed it in an interview with me,

> I think there are different kinds of belief. My belief in God has in general been derived from experiences with God. My belief in the basic stories of science have been based upon argument and evidence. To me my faith comes from subjective experiences in prayer, reading scripture, and in conversations with

others who have had similar subjective encounters with God. The evidence about God comes from within, while my knowledge of science comes from objective information.

And these are just a few of the potentially endless number of examples of belief that put the lie to the notion that fundamentalists are somehow representative of how to believe. The irony is that, as I've attempted to show, fundamentalists of all stripes, whether openly religious or ostensibly irreligious, are far closer to one another in their basic attitude toward the world than are the agnostic and moderately religious.

Let's say you are Richard Dawkins, Sam Harris, or any of the authors I discussed at the beginning of this book. If you espouse their kind of radical or nonpluralistic atheism, you'll need to argue that the hypothesis that there is a God is a claim like any other and should be considered on its merits, based on the existing evidence. The evidence, you'll go on to say, is overwhelmingly in favor of there being no God. This seems totally straightforward. What could possibly be fundamentalist about such a position? To begin with, the sense of total certainty that someone like Dawkins evinces simply echoes how fundamentalists sound when they talk about their beliefs. As Alister and Joanna McGrath have put it, "The total dogmatic conviction of correctness which pervades some sections of Western atheism today—wonderfully illustrated by *The God Delusion*—immediately aligns it with a religious fundamentalism that refuses to allow its ideas to be examined or challenged."

But Dawkins's form of fundamentalism is not merely a question of style. His position is fundamentalist because it assumes not merely that individual hypotheses about this or that cause or effect are subject to verification but also that hypotheses about *the totality of being* as it is in itself are also subject to verification and hence to being *known*. But once you assume that everything *can* be known— that is, that everything in the past, the present, and also the future has the attribute of being knowable as it is in itself—then you have just accepted the most basic of fundamentalist principles. Since only an omniscient being could know the entirety of the world without the limitations imposed by having a body and using a medium, the atheist has also implicitly and necessarily presupposed a God-like knowledge and made himself heir to that knowledge. In other words, stating with absolute confidence that God does not exist, or even putting the hypothesis that God exists on the same level as normal, verifiable hypotheses, assumes as possible a knowledge that only something the God of the monotheistic traditions could have.

The atheist, then, is religious, and the kind of religion shared by both atheists and religious fundamentalists is the religion of arrogance. The religion of arrogance is arrogant because it presumes that there can be knowledge of, at least in theory, the totality of existence. It presumes, in other words, to say something definitive about something that human knowledge cannot in fact know, namely, the totality of the universe as it is in itself. As I have been arguing in this book, however, the religion of arrogance is not the only possible religious stance. Opposed to it is the moderate attitude, which we could call the religion of humility. The religion of humility is not at all religious in the same way that atheists and other adherents of the religion of arrogance are. Instead, the religion of humility understands that human beings, trapped by the limitations of space and time, cannot possibly have perfect knowledge of a totality that encompasses all space and time. Something, in other words, always escapes human knowledge. This is not the same, to be sure, as affirming that there is Some Thing or Supreme Being that escapes human knowledge; rather, it affirms merely that human knowledge is essentially and by definition limited.

This religion of humility is thus also religious but only in the sense that it recognizes, by necessity, the possibility of something else, of something that transcends the limits of human understanding. It may even refer to that something as God, and it may pose theological questions intent on exploring the limits of human knowledge. But it will never presume to speak with certainty about what transcends those limits, for to do so is to speak the language of arrogance. This religion of humility is what is shared by all those of what Wolfe calls quiet faith; it is an uncertain faith, the religious moderation that I find not only philosophically justified but also in some senses the best defense against fundamentalisms of all kinds.

I have insisted at several points in this book that the arguments I present here are philosophical in nature. What I mean by that is that they do not assume any religious creed or dogma as a starting point. In that sense, I think I have a stronger position to argue with someone like Sam Harris than does Andrew Sullivan, as much as I often admire his writings. Unlike me, when Sullivan debates a point with an atheist critic, he tends to fall back on positions that only other Christians would accept, which has the predictable effect of closing down dialogue with his opponent rather than enabling anything like common ground.

I am convinced this common ground exists, at least with some of the new atheists. Harris, for example, has rejected the term *atheist* and has at times taken an explicitly agnostic position, despite the vehemence of his earlier positions. As I mentioned, I am largely in agreement with many if not most of their criticisms of religion, with the caveat that they are really pertinent to fundamentalism, not religion per se. But if I do not explicitly assume any religious position, is it not the case that I am nonetheless arguing from a religious position? What authority do I have to try to arbitrate between believers and nonbelievers? What authority would anyone have, for that matter, as it would seem to be a debate with no middle ground?

So it seems that after all these pages, at least some introduction is in order. I was raised Roman Catholic and have received all the sacraments a lay Catholic can be expected to receive (excluding, I am pleased to say, extreme unction). My mother comes from a New York Irish Catholic family and still attends mass weekly. My father is an Episcopalian who on sunny days would stay behind when my mother and I went to mass, saying God was as likely to be out in the garden as in a stuffy church. He has remarried, and though he attends church more regularly now, it hasn't stopped him from believing that God is a socialist who enjoys a good game of tennis on a hot day followed by a few cold beers.

Somewhere along the way from childhood to adulthood, and perhaps in the same way children stop believing in Santa, I stopped believing in the literal existence of God, the either kindly or fiery image of a white-bearded superbeing like the one stretching out his finger to Adam across the ceiling of the Sistine Chapel. I stopped attending mass regularly and became very angry with the Church over its intransigent policies against contraception and a woman's right to choose. I also came to learn, before ever reaching the point of openly abandoning my religious affiliation, that there are many Catholics who feel and think the same way as I do, in open defiance of official Church teaching—this, it's worth mentioning, in an organization that is supposedly a theocracy run by an all-powerful dictator. (This can be for bad or for good. As Sam Harris points out, 74 percent of Americans disagree with the Church's teaching that capital punishment is wrong—which negates his claim that one either accepts the dictates of a given religion whole hog or not at all.) I learned early on from benevolent and at times brilliant priests (and I know this was very much the luck of the draw) that believing in God need not be the same as believing that 2 + 2 = 4 or that life on earth is carbon based. When the priest teaching Sunday school at Saint Agnes's church in Arlington, Virginia, where I lived during middle and high school, said it was natural to doubt that the little plastic-tasting wafers they give out for Communion in the modern mass was really the body of God, he was really quite understanding when I countered that it was just as difficult to believe it was a piece of bread.

I am married to an Austrian woman who, like most Austrians, was also raised a Catholic. As in my case, her mother was a Catholic who practiced her religion and her father a Protestant who did not. My mother-in-law, to whose memory I have dedicated this book and who witnessed her grandmother being shot during the Nazi period after a neighbor denounced her as a Jew, studied philosophy and theology into her later life, and carried on a correspondence with Elie Wiesel about Christian guilt and the Holocaust. My wife's older brother (the one from the casino anecdote so many chapters back) was serious enough about his religion to have studied to be a priest, although now he has his own family and owns some hip bars and art house cinemas in Vienna instead. One of my wife's other brothers professes no religion and lives on the Cape Verde Islands with his Cape Verdean wife and children, where he has established a community center for the local youth. My wife's oldest sister married a man from Sudan, converted to Islam, and now raises her children as Muslims, although she has been divorced from their father for several years. She wears a veil and prays toward Mecca five times a day. As I write this chapter we are on vacation together in Croatia, where our local version of the

Clash of Civilizations involves our children playing together late into the evening while we enjoy hours of conversation.

These conversations need not end in agreement. One recent evening my Muslim sister-in-law, Ange, mentioned in passing that her friend's husband was taking a second wife and that this was causing her friend some stress. This passing comment initiated a storm of debate, with my other sister-in-law remarking that whatever religious reasons the husband may have had, the real motivation was that he wanted to have sex with a new, younger woman. Ange became defensive and started justifying her own acceptance of the practice of polygamy on the fact that God made the sexes different and made women subservient to men. Johannes—the brother-in-law who had earlier studied to be a priest—countered that God had no interest in human sexual relations and that the minute religions started using God to justify established social customs they were essentially out of bounds.

Johannes, I think, hit the nail on the head. To the extent that Ange based her willingness to adapt to certain customs on a belief that she knew (or believed that Islam knew) God's will on a certain matter, she was taking a fundamentalist position. Johannes, for his part, in his refusal to countenance such an argument was responding from a moderate's position. The debate, in other words, wasn't so much one between religions as one between two different ways of being religious.

The Barriers of Evidence

My daughter started expressing dismay about death (certainly the origin of all religious questions) when she was around four years old. She is preparing for First Communion next year, something my oldest son did himself two years ago. There is no doubt that our decision to baptize and raise our children as Catholics puts my wife and me on Sam Harris's list of aiders and abettors, and yet I find it far more important whether I raise my children as fundamentalists than whether I raise them as religious or not. When my son asks, as he does with some frequency, about the origins of the world or of human beings, or about where our loved ones are now that they have died, I tell him, respectively, what I know about cosmology and evolution and that we don't have the same kinds of answers for those big questions. I also tell him about Christian belief in and hope for eternal life but always stressing that these are stories about those areas of life that science cannot explain and has no interest in. Religion and science have so far encountered no conflict in my son's education.

My own Catholic upbringing did involve some perhaps unnecessary hand-wringing about impure thoughts as well as some deep consideration of the morality of abortion (both rather quickly decided, the one in favor of the permissibility of impurity, the other of a woman's unfettered right to choose). But the Testament's stories, New and Old, never once put the brakes on my fascination with the workings of science and the world of ideas. In fact, the existence in my life of a realm of counterintuitive stories making implausible claims to truth may well have strengthened rather than weakened my commitment to seek the truth in this world.

Humans have a well-known tendency to rationalize, that is, to try to make reasonable a course of life or thought that they are currently engaged in and to do so until some insurmountable barrier arises that makes that course so obviously wrong (not only to others but to themselves as well) that they must finally back up and take another route. This tendency is at work, I would insist, in every manner of life or thought, religious or secular. The atheists who attack religion note, and not without justification, that one of the principal sins of religion is that it makes the insurmountable barriers of evidence that much more surmountable, just as Don Quixote was armed with an imaginary nemesis who allowed him to chalk up to evil enchantments each and every intrusion of physical reality into his fantasies. But what these well-intentioned critics fail to see is that reason has its own, even more subtle ladders with which to clamber over those pesky barriers. For often what we take to be the purity of reason is nothing other than the time-honored dedication to a dogma that has escaped notice as such, largely by being cloaked in the guise of reason.

On March 7, 1277, probably acting in response to an inquiry into heretical views at the university of Paris by Pope John XXI, Stephen Tempier, the bishop of Paris, published a condemnation of 219 philosophical and theological teachings he believed to be common within the faculty of arts. At the core of the condemnation was an explicit series of articles prohibiting scholars from positing that God's power was limited in any way. The curious effect of this—from our perspective unconscionable—limitation of freedom of thought was that suddenly a generation of scholars was able to throw off the sedimentation of years of Aristotelian reason and make exciting advances in the discovery of nature's laws. Until then, for instance, it had been accepted as creed that God could not possibly move the universe given that Aristotle's logic defined movement as a change of place and place as the relation between a contained and a container. Something as all encompassing as the cosmos could not possibly have a container and, ergo, could not possibly move, no matter what God said to the contrary.

The Church's motives were clearly not directed toward the preservation of academic freedom when the condemnation of 1277 was issued; the result of the official limitation, however, was an explosion of speculation concerning the shape, boundaries, and movement of the cosmos that propelled scientific inquiry rather than hampered it. This event of 1277 is an example of a productive tension, in other words, between science and religion, and it is far from an isolated one. Isaac Newton was not only a firm (some might say fanatic) observer of the Puritan faith (the fringe fundamentalists of their own time) but also a fervent alchemist who took his search for the philosopher's stone as seriously as his work on mathematics and the basic forces of the universe. While Newton's theory of gravity was the single most accurate scientific description of one of the universe's basic forces until Einstein's general theory of relativity overturned it, it was looked upon with suspicion by some of Newton's more rationally inclined colleagues, who felt a theory about unseen forces smacked of magic.

It is easy to speak from the vantage of hindsight and claim that Newton and legions of other scientists, authors, and artists would have been more brilliant, more creative had they not been hampered by the unnecessary burdens of their superstitions and faith, but the empirical evidence that atheists are supposed to so respect certainly speaks otherwise. Even Einstein, who did not believe "in a personal God" and publicly corrected the widespread idea that he did, did believe that God was present in the beauty and order of the universe whose laws he was discovering, and, hence, like so many other cosmologists his search was in some sense oriented toward the divine.

As a general rule, beneficial effects may indeed spring from the existence of a personal realm of beliefs making unreasonable claims on gray matter otherwise entirely dedicated to reason or entirely led by custom. What religious dicta can do in such circumstances, when in tension with the certainties of reason or unquestioned social habits, is cause one to pause and consider. I would claim that a believer in a woman's right to choose who has come to that conclusion—as many Catholics have—after seriously contemplating the claim that a fetus is a life, even if only a potential one, is more dedicated, more passionate, and better armed to argue the case than one whose belief simply emerged from a social context without facing any serious challenge. In a similar way, one's moral universe may be better served by hard-won battles against apparently needless prohibitions than by painting every moral decision as a forgone conclusion. Our very existence is organized around breaking the Ten Commandments, as the French psychoanalyst Jacques Lacan once pointed out, a fact that upholds rather than diminishes their importance in our social life.

But it is also important to recognize that religion's social prohibitions are not games. The prohibition on masturbation may well have, as Christopher Hitchens has claimed, wreaked havoc on the minds and morals of countless youth who have suffered to take it seriously; and the disastrous separation of Islamic youth from any sexual release or contact until adulthood has almost certainly helped fuel the potential for violence among both Palestinians forced to feel the daily humiliation of Israeli security checkpoints and Afghan boys subjected to the mindless drumming of the Taliban madrassas. As Hitchens reiterates with some vehemence, it's not the virgins that await them in heaven that are the problem; the problem is that they *are* virgins.

Likewise the Catholic Church's disastrous stance on such issues as abortion and, most extremely, contraception has been responsible for extraordinary suffering and death, which fact alone clearly makes the line I am treading most tenuous; indeed, it is far easier to adopt any extreme than to explore such shaky middle ground. Willingness to consider religious prohibitions in the area of reproductive rights works for a moderate only because a moderate, no matter what he decides in his own life, will stop short of agreeing that such prohibitions be imposed on other people. The desire to impose moral certainties on others in the form of law requires a kind of dogmatic certainty that moderates, with their built-in suspicion of the code of codes, simply do not have. The theocratic governments of Nicaragua and El Salvador that have arisen out of U.S. interventions there have turned Church doctrine into a nightmare regime of back-alley abortions and life sentences for desperate girls, even victims of rape and incest. But this is the doing of organized fundamentalism, not just religion. A similar holocaust for baby girls has gone on undisturbed for years in China, where state-imposed limitations on reproduction have nothing to do with religious dogma. And while Christian opposition to sex education and condoms has been an unspeakable evil in the age of HIV, it is an evil wrought by fundamentalism, for no moderate would ever put his own religious belief above the obvious suffering and death of other people.

The difference between fundamentalism and moderation, in other words, is not one of degree but of kind. Therefore, though it is true that prohibitions in the hands and minds of fundamentalists are dangerous and can be highly damaging, both socially and psychically, the problem is not the prohibition but the mentality of those issuing it and internalizing it. The great historian and political theorist Michel Foucault was famously ambivalent about the liberalizing of sexual mores that would eventually assimilate gay men into normal, middle-class, conformist existence; because something about the outlaw status of being gay in the 1970s was essential to his relationship with his sexuality—and this in full recognition of the suffering and death that this prohibition had, in the hands of fundamentalists, already produced.

The moderate's attitude toward the prohibitions that make up either his or her religious code or social reality is tentative, experimental, and selective. On the one hand, the moderate is open to the possibility that a given prohibition is simply evil and must be resisted. This is the case with many Catholics who have long ignored the Church's ban on contraception in their own lives and who now openly oppose it. On the other hand, the moderate recognizes some prohibitions as either producing some social benefit or adding in some way to life's texture and beauty. Certainly the nudity prohibition is as ludicrous at times as it is historically variable. The bared breasts on the cover of *National Geographic* that aroused generations of Western boys did not likely have the same effect in their own cultures, and Freud transmits faithfully the embarrassment of a nobleman whose dream that he had been indecently exposed involved his being seen on the street without his sword.

For this very reason the line of the décolletage or the height of the hem has always been a culture's libidinal borderline, moving up and down as the time demanded and leaving a surplus of sublimated pleasure in its wake. What would Western literature be without the little curtain hiding our view of Madame Bovary's coach ride, and this despite or perhaps because of the indignity of the indecency charges that Flaubert was made to endure. Indeed an artist's job is perhaps nothing other than to explore those boundaries in the aesthetic realm, and I have no doubt that there would be very little left of aesthetics if we could (which we can't) do away with those boundaries altogether.

Ultimately what religion with its prohibitions asks of us, however, is that we balance or mitigate the satisfaction of our immediate desires by focusing, at times, on something *else*, something that exceeds the realm of our physical needs, pleasures, and understanding. Atheists may claim that social prohibitions and rules as well as an innate sense of ethics already do that, but I am not convinced. The atheists writing today share an unfettered and for the most part unexamined prejudice for the Western and even U.S. model of the individual. The individual's desires are at the center of how the market works; his or her freedom is supposedly what is at stake in politics; and his or her rights are at the heart of the judicial system. This individual seems to have undergone a kind of parthenogenic birth, devoid of history of any kind, as when Sam Harris marvels that humans could have been stupid enough for so much of their history as not to notice that religion's edicts are wrong and that its moral principles are lacking. As he puts it with regard to slavery,

> The moment a person recognizes that slaves are human
> beings like himself, enjoying the same capacity for suffering

and happiness, he will understand that it is patently evil to own them and treat them like farm equipment. It is remarkably easy for a person to arrive at this epiphany—and yet, it had to be spread at the point of a bayonet throughout the Confederate South, among the most pious Christians the country has ever known.

It is breathtaking what little thought and how little historical consciousness go into a declaration like this, about how "remarkably easy" it is to see the evil of slavery. Of course it is remarkably easy for us, here, now, from the wisdom of a hindsight that has enjoyed thousands of years of (often theological) debate on the nature of the human soul and the legality of humans owning other humans. It is remarkably easy indeed, once one has been bequeathed the idea of the modern individual, decked out in his unalienable rights and further clarified by generations of legal interpretations and civic struggle. But the same historical blindness allows the atheist to forget that this abstract and legal entity may itself impose certain limitations on our vision and knowledge. Religion's value in modern times, and for a moderate mind-set, can also be to turn our attention away from the ego's constant demands. By giving of our time, energy, and goods to a community, and by giving over our thoughts to the ineffable, we may weaken, if only slightly, the ego's extraordinary grip, a grip that has made ours the most self-obsessed society ever to grace the world with its presence.

Moderate Belief

Atheists get a lot of mileage out of claims that 80 percent of the U.S. population, for instance, believes that the Second Coming is imminent (a ludicrous claim, as I've shown, but that doesn't stop it from being bandied about). But only fundamentalists, whether religious or secular, would insist that everything one "believes" must be believed in the same way. Moderates live in a very different world, a world in which there are multiple beliefs and many different ways to believe in them. For a fundamentalist, the belief in the virgin birth of Jesus can be understood only on the level of a belief that the earth revolves around the sun (or vice versa, to make the analogy more accurate). A moderate, on the other hand, understands that beliefs of a metaphysical nature have nothing to do with the respect one grants science; moreover, granting metaphysical speculation its own autonomous space helps ensure that scientific inquiry remains unmuddled by reason's grandiose propensity to engrave its own certainties in stone.

Atheists like Sam Harris continually accuse religious moderates of cherry picking the Bible for truths they see fit to believe in, an accusation shared by religious fundamentalists as well. In fact, both the religious and the irreligious fundamentalists are openly at one in this regard; they cast occasional glances of mutual admiration at each other and pat each other's backs at their moral superiority over backsliding, wishy-washy moderates. But this agreement is more than a mere coincidence. Atheists and religious fundamentalists admire each other so fervently because they are cut of the same cloth. What neither understands is that cherry picking is the essence of both biblical scholarship (the kind that leads to religion's own critique of its own doctrines) *and* empirical science. How can you claim to be an advocate of the scientific method while accusing others of cherry picking? The scientific method is nothing other than the institutionalization of cherry picking as a general attitude toward the world! Cherry picking, in other words, means sticking with what works and rejecting the rest. In the realm of science it means posing theories, testing them, and altering them based on those results. In the realm of religion it means adopting certain passages of scripture and teachings for their life lessons and rejecting others as inadmissible. You think that's a violation of your creed? That's because you're a fundamentalist. Moderates do it all the time.

While atheists and fundamentalists detest moderates for the wishy-washiness of their beliefs, their own fervor is that of a convert's faith, or a recent immigrant's patriotism. At times there is something distinctly American in this phenomenon, where evangelicals ask one another when they were saved by Jesus and one side of a debate rails against the other for its lies and disingenuousness. A moderate's faith is more relaxed, more natural. In fact, it makes more sense to picture this faith in terms of an identity than a creed. A moderate identifies with a community because that community in some sense represents his or her origins, his or her history. There is no more reason for a moderate Catholic to believe a Jew is wrong about his faith than there is for an Irishman to believe an Italian is wrong about her nationality. Like ethnic identities, faiths are composed of practices, stories, rituals, and rote behavior. They can be learned, over time, and even changed, but only with difficulty. That is why American evangelism is so strange to so many Europeans, the same people whom Christopher Hitchens praises as being the least religious people in the world. It is not that modern Europeans are less religious than others, though; they are merely less fundamentalist, for their long history has taught them that faith and nationality are to be valued as peaceful attributes, but that when used as the fodder of war they lead only to internecine destruction.

In the end, we are all agnostic. Some of us are aware of this, and some are not. We are agnostic because, quite simply, we cannot know. We can know the world as it appears to us; we can measure it with remarkable accuracy; we can predict outcomes and effects; we can explain many of its myriad and wonderful phenomena; we cannot, however, know it in its totality, as it is in itself. We cannot know if there is something like God, and we cannot know what it would be like for such a God, if one exists, to know the world. This is a fact. Fundamentalists and atheists refuse to accept this fact. If they do, they are neither fundamentalists nor atheists but moderates and agnostics. Religious moderation is, in other words, a kind of agnosticism. It is an agnosticism that decides to believe in—not to know—something that it knows it cannot know.

Atheists make a lot of hay out of a very simple sounding point. When it comes to truth claims, either you're right or you're wrong. There is no in between. So, either the Christian Nation to whom Sam Harris writes his letter is right that Jesus is its personal savior and Harris will be going to hell for his disbelief, or it is wrong and either some other version of religion or Harris's own atheism gets the story right. This sound, rational assumption—either there is a God or there isn't—however, holds water only if the fundamentalist logic of the code of codes is true.

There is a story that nicely illustrates my point here. In the story— which has been attributed to Jain, Buddhist, Sufi, and Hindu wisdom—

some blind men encounter an elephant and each opines on what they have before them. The one feeling its trunk says it's a tree, the one touching its tail says a length of rope, and so on. To make the analogy to religion clearer, we might add that they go on to have progeny who then fight and kill one another over their clans' various interpretations, but the meaning of the tale is the same. It's simply not the case that the blind men's interpretations are mutually exclusive, since they were only ever partial to begin with.

Where the story fails as an analogy is that we the listeners are told from the outset that the object in question is an elephant. We don't share the blindness, in other words, and hence are in a position of implicit condescension toward the blind men. This might well be described as the atheist's position, one from which he sees that the elephant is simply an elephant, or that the emperor has no clothes. The problem is that, as I have shown in this book, in the case of metaphysical claims about the nature of everything—which are the very purpose of religions—there is absolutely nothing we can say about the elephant because whatever it is, it exceeds in principle the capacities of human knowledge. In fact, the elephant can be grasped only as an object of knowledge, as an "elephant," if we have accepted and internalized the false logic of the code of codes.

According to this logic, the ultimate nature of the world can be grasped as an object of knowledge precisely because it encodes the world we grasp with our senses. To continue with the analogy provided by the blind men, the object they fail to grasp has a form that their eventual efforts, conversation, or addition of further sensory abilities will enable them to perceive and recognize. The cognizable object of "elephant" lies behind the partial experience of "tree" and "rope" as their ultimate code. In the case of the ultimate nature of everything, however, such knowledge is absolutely impossible. The total universe as an object of knowledge is utterly beyond not only our grasp but also grasping per se, because grasping it *as it is in itself* would entail an eradication of the very successiveness of time and externality of space that are essential to grasping something, seeing something, or knowing something in the first place.

Once we have accepted that the code of codes is an illusion, it becomes patently clear that not only can religious disputes not be arbitrated but also that there is no reason whatsoever that apparently competing truth claims must be mutually exclusive. From a moderate's perspective, his own attachment to a community that believes in a God who became human in the form of his own son conceived of a virgin says nothing at all about another believer's conviction that God revealed his will to a forty-year-old man in a mountain cave or another's belief that the Messiah is yet to come. To the religious moderate, it is natural that these stories differ and even that they appear to contradict one another, for each is and cannot be other than a blind man's interpretation of an elephant.

In the end, not only do religions not contradict one another, but in some profound way religion's exigency to believe in impossible theories, much ridiculed by atheists, is at the very heart of its purpose. What religion in its various forms attests to is the ungraspable nature of metaphysical knowledge. Thus there can be no greater logic than the illogical, paradoxical claims of creeds to believe in the virgin birth of God or to admire as a model of faith the inconceivable willingness of a man to sacrifice his own son to a faceless God. These stories testify above all to a knowledge of utmost importance for humans to grasp, namely, the knowledge that our own knowledge, as grandiose and wondrous as it is, is bounded in its very nature in ways we can never surpass.

Countless people around the world baptize their children, attend bat mitzvahs, and observe high holidays without ever taking their participation in these practices to mean that the religions of others or the discoveries of science must be false. In large measure these people are tolerant, cosmopolitan, and peace loving. Nevertheless, if there's one aspect that all recent attacks on religion have in common, it's the venom with which they berate these religious moderates. According to these attacks, if religious fanatics are the war criminals responsible for the downfall of modern civilization, moderates—the people David Brooks refers to as the quasi-religious—are their silent collaborators. In that light, perhaps the most important conclusion to draw from my discussion of the code of codes is that it is these quasi-religious, those who humbly refuse to speak with certainty on matters outside the ken of human knowledge, who are in the right. The worldview of a moderately religious Catholic, Muslim, or Jew not only is more likely to foster tolerance, peace, and social justice than the worldview of the religious fanatic or his atheist antagonist, but is also the philosophically and scientifically more rigorous position. In their refusal to believe in the code of codes—in their reluctance, in other words, to act as if the ultimate reality were already written in a language they can understand and thus to condemn other practices as contravening that knowledge—the practicing scientists, the moderate believers, and the adherents of the religion of humility all defend a worldview that affirms freedom, the quest for truth, and the betterment of life as the core values of being human.

Selected Bibliography and Recommended Reading

The works that follow have either been cited in the text or were indispensable to my research. General knowledge about events reported in newspapers, for example, has not been referenced unless an article was directly quoted; nor do I reference films or television series other than by title in the text. I reference quotations from Internet sources along with the date they were last accessed. Finally, a source that I cite in more than one chapter is referenced only in the earlier chapter.

Introduction: An Uncertain Faith

Dawkins, Richard. *The God Delusion*. New York: Houghton Mifflin, 2006.

Harris, Sam. *The End of Faith: Religion, Terror, and the Future of Reason*. New York: Norton, 2004.

——. *Letter to a Christian Nation*. New York: Knopf, 2006.

——. "The Problem with Atheism." Lecture given in Washington, D.C., in 2007. http://newsweek.washingtonpost.com/onfaith/panelists/sam_harris/2007/10/the_problem_with_atheism.html (accessed January 29, 2010).

Hitchens, Christopher. *God Is Not Great: How Religion Poisons Everything*. New York: Twelve Books, 2007.

Newberg, Andrew, and Mark Robert Waldman. *Why We Believe What We Believe: Uncovering Our Biological Need for Meaning, Spirituality, and Truth*. New York: Free Press, 2006.

Nussbaum, Martha. *Liberty of Conscience: In Defense of America's Tradition of Religious Equality*. New York: Basic Books, 2008.

Penrose, Roger. *The Road to Reality: A Complete Guide to the Laws of the Universe*. New York: Knopf, 2005.

Wittgenstein, Ludwig. *On Certainty*. Edited by G. E. M. Anscombe and G. H. von Wright. Translated by Denis Paul and G. E. M. Anscombe. Oxford: Blackwell, 1975.

1. Dogmatic Atheism

Agee, Joel. Quoted in Up Front, arts section of the *New York Times*, April 15, 2007. http://query.nytimes.com/gst/fullpage.html?res=9404E0DF143FF 936A25757C0A9619C8B63 (accessed January 29, 2010).

Alexander, Matthew. *How to Break a Terrorist: The U.S. Interrogators Who Used Brains, Not Brutality, to Take Down the Deadliest Man in Iraq.* New York: Free Press, 2008.

Atran, Scott. *In Gods We Trust: The Evolutionary Landscape of Religion.* New York: Oxford University Press, 2002.

Behe, Michael J. *Darwin's Black Box: The Biochemical Challenge to Evolution.* New York: Free Press, 2006.

Boyer, Pascal. *Religion Explained: The Human Instinct That Fashions Gods, Spirits, and Ancestors.* London: Heinemann, 2001.

Dennett, Daniel C. *Breaking the Spell: Religion as a Natural Phenomenon.* New York: Viking, 2006.

Harris, Sam, J. T. Kaplan, A. Curiel, S. Y. Bookheimer, M. Iacoboni, M. S. Cohen. "The Neural Correlates of Religious and Nonreligious Belief." *PLoS ONE* 4, no. 10 (2009): e7272.

Haught, John F. *God and the New Atheists: A Critical Response to Dawkins, Harris, and Hitchens.* Louisville, Ky.: Westminster John Knox Press, 2008.

Hitchens, Christopher. "Believe Me, It's Torture." *Vanity Fair*, August 2008. http://www.vanityfair.com/politics/features/2008/08/hitchens200808 (accessed January 29, 2010).

Jeffrey, Grant R. *Creation: Remarkable Evidence of God's Design.* Colorado Springs, Colo.: WaterBrook Press, 2003.

——. *The Next World War: What Prophecy Reveals About Extreme Islam and the West.* Colorado Springs, Colo.: WaterBrook Press, 2006.

Sayre, Kenneth M. *Belief and Knowledge: Mapping the Cognitive Landscape.* Lanham, Md.: Rowman & Littlefield, 1997.

Tkacz, Michael W. "Thomas Aquinas vs. the Intelligent Designers: What Is God's Finger Doing in My Pre-Biotic Soup?" http://guweb2.gonzaga.edu/ faculty/calhoun/socratic/Tkacz_AquinasvsID.html (accessed January 29, 2010).

2. The Fundamentalism of Everyday Life

Appiah, K. Anthony. *In My Father's House: Africa in the Philosophy of Culture.* Oxford: Oxford University Press, 1992.

Boa, Kenneth, and John Alan Turner. *The Gospel According to the Da Vinci Code: The Truth Behind the Writings of Dan Brown*. Nashville, Tenn.: Broadman and Holman, 2006.

Borges, Jorge Luis. *Ficciones*. Translated by Anthony Bonner. New York: Grove Press, 1962.

Brown, Dan. *The Da Vinci Code*. New York: Anchor, 2003.

Byrne, Rhonda. *The Secret*. New York: Atria, 2006.

D'Souza, Dinesh. *The End of Racism: Principles for a Multiracial Society*. New York: Free Press, 1995.

Elliott, Carl. *Better Than Well: American Medicine Meets the American Dream*. New York: Norton, 2003.

Gladwell, Malcolm. *Blink: The Power of Thinking Without Thinking*. New York: Little, Brown, 2005.

Greene, Brian. *The Fabric of the Cosmos: Space, Time, and the Texture of Reality*. New York: Knopf, 2004.

Herbert, Bob. "Arrested While Grieving." *New York Times*, May 26, 2007. http://query.nytimes.com/gst/fullpage.html?res=9F0DEFDD1730F935A1 5756C0A9619C8B63 (accessed January 29, 2010).

Kristof, Nicholas. "More Schools, Not Troops." *New York Times*, October 29, 2009. http://www.nytimes.com/2009/10/29/opinion/29kristof.html?_ r=2 (accessed January 30, 2010).

Lahaye, Tim, and Jerry B. Jenkins. *Left Behind*. Carol Stream, Ill.: Tyndale House, 1995.

Las Casas, Bartolomé de. *In Defense of the Indians*. Translated by Stafford Poole. DeKalb: Northern Illinois University Press, 1992.

Leibniz, Gottfried Wilhelm. *The Monadology*. Translated by Robert Latta. Oxford: Clarendon Press, 1898. Also available online at http://philosophy. eserver.org/leibniz-monadology.txt (accessed on January 30, 2010).

Longman, Jeré. "An Amputee Sprinter: Is He Disabled or Too-Abled?" *New York Times*, May 15, 2007. http://www.nytimes.com/2007/05/15/sports/ othersports/15runner.html (accessed January 29, 2010).

Maryland Court of Special Appeals. Petition and Brief of *Amici Curiae*, Citizens for Traditional Families, Family Leader Foundation, and United Families International in Support of Defendants-Appellants Frank Conaway, et al., Defendants-Appellants vs. Gitanjali Deane, et al., Plaintiffs-Appellees, no. 02499, September Term, 2005.

Maryland Court of Special Appeals. Petition and Brief *Amicus Curiae* of The Knights of Columbus in Support of Defendants-Appellants Frank Conaway, et al., Defendants-Appellants vs. Gitanjali Deane, et al., Plaintiffs-Appellees, no. 02499, September Term, 2005.

Mencken, H. L. "Obituary for William Jennings Bryan." *Baltimore Evening Sun*, July 27, 1925.

"Obama, the American Left, and Political Agency." Blog posting at *Below the Belt*, November 17, 2008. http://feed.belowthebelt.org/2008/11/obama-american-left-and-political.html (accessed January 30, 2010).

Obama, Barack. *The Audacity of Hope: Thoughts on Reclaiming the American Dream*. New York: Three Rivers Press, 2006.

Rorty, Richard. *Take Care of Freedom and Truth Will Take Care of Itself: Interviews with Richard Rorty*. Edited by Eduardo Mendieta. Stanford, Calif.: Stanford University Press, 2006.

Rowling, J. K. *Harry Potter and the Order of the Phoenix*. New York: Scholastic, 2004.

Somerville, Margaret A. "The Case Against 'Same-Sex Marriage.'" A Brief Submitted to the Standing Committee on Justice and Human Rights. www.marriageinstitute.ca/images/somerville.pdf (accessed January 30, 2010).

Spooner, Lysander. "Natural Law or the Science of Justice: A Treatise on Natural Law, Natural Justice, Natural Rights, Natural Liberty, and Natural Society; Showing That All Legislation Whatsoever Is an Absurdity, a Usurpation, and a Crime." Available online at http://www.panarchy.org/spooner/law.1882.html (accessed January 30, 2010).

Waldman, Amy. "Prophetic Justice." *Atlantic*, October 2006. http://www.theatlantic.com/doc/200610/waldman-islam (accessed January 29, 2010).

Warren, Rick. *The Purpose-Driven Life: What on Earth Am I Here For?* Grand Rapids, Mich.: Zondervan, 2007.

Weber, Brenda. "Makeover as Takeover: Scenes of Affective Domination on Makeover TV." *Configurations* 15, no. 1 (2007): 77–100.

Žižek, Slavoj. "The Depraved Heroes of *24* Are the Himmlers of Hollywood." *Guardian*, January 10, 2006.

3. The Language of God

Abou El Fadl, Khaled. *The Place of Tolerance in Islam*. Boston: Beacon Press, 2002.

Alighieri, Dante. *De vulgari eloquentia*. Available online at http://www.theorb.net/encyclop/culture/lit/italian/da_e.htm#op_dve (accessed January 30, 2010).

Armstrong, Karen. *The Battle for God*. New York: Knopf, 2000.

——. *The Case for God*. New York: Knopf, 2009.

———. *The Great Transformation: The Beginning of Our Religious Traditions.* New York: Knopf, 2006.

———. *Islam: A Short History.* New York: Modern Library, 2000.

Augustine. *The City of God Against the Pagans.* Edited by A. W. Dyson. Cambridge: Cambridge University Press, 1998.

———. *On Genesis.* Translated by Edmund Hill. New York: New City Press, 2002.

Bono, James J. *The Word of God and the Languages of Man: Interpreting Nature in Early Modern Science and Medicine.* Madison: University of Wisconsin Press, 1995.

Buruma, Ian. *Taming the Gods: Religion and Democracy on Three Continents.* Princeton, N.J.: Princeton University Press, 2010.

Collins, Francis S. *The Language of God: A Scientist Presents Evidence for Belief.* New York: Free Press, 2006.

Eco, Umberto. *The Search for the Perfect Language.* Translated by James Fentress. Malden, Mass.: Blackwell, 1997.

———. *Serendipities: Language and Lunacy.* Translated by William Weaver. New York: Columbia University Press, 1998.

Isidore of Seville, Saint. *The "Etymologies" of Isidore of Seville.* Translated by Stephen A. Barney, W. J. Lewis, J. A. Beach, and Oliver Berghof. Cambridge: Cambridge University Press, 2006.

Johnson, David E. "Idiocy, the Name of God." Unpublished essay.

Kant, Immanuel. *Critique of Pure Reason.* Translated and edited by Paul Guyer and Allen W. Wood. Cambridge: Cambridge University Press, 1998.

Lewis, Bernard. *The Crisis of Islam: Holy War and Unholy Terror.* New York: Modern Library, 2003.

Lilla, Mark. *The Stillborn God: Religion, Politics, and the Modern West.* New York: Knopf, 2007.

Maimonides, Moses. *The Guide for the Perplexed.* Translated by M. Friedländer. New York: Dover, 1956.

Marty, Martin E., and R. Scott Appleby. *The Fundamentalism Project.* 6 vols. Chicago: University of Chicago Press, 1993–2004.

Plato. *Complete Works.* Edited by John M. Cooper. Indianapolis: Hackett, 1997.

Plotinus. *The Six Enneads.* Translated by Stephen Mackenna and B. S. Page. Available online at http://classics.mit.edu/Plotinus/enneads.html (accessed January 30, 2010).

Sefer Yetzirah: The Book of Creation. Translated by Aryeh Kaplan. York Beach, Maine: Red Wheel, 1997.

Taylor, Charles. *A Secular Age.* Cambridge, Mass.: Harvard University Press, 2007.

Thomas Aquinas, Saint. *Summa theologica.* Available online at http://www. ccel.org/ccel/aquinas/summa/home.html (accessed January 20, 2010).

4. Faith in Science

Brockman, John. "Introduction: The Emerging Third Culture." In *The Third Culture.* New York: Simon and Schuster, 1996.

Brownback, Sam. "What I Think About Evolution." *New York Times*, May 31, 2007. http://www.nytimes.com/2007/05/31/opinion/31brownback.html (accessed January 31, 2010).

Catalano, Peter. "A Dose of Reality Emerges in L.A." *Los Angeles Times*, November 28, 1991. http://www.brockman.com/press/1991.11.28.latimes. html (accessed January 31, 2010).

Dennett, Daniel C. *Consciousness Explained.* New York: Little, Brown, 1991.

Gingerich, Owen. *God's Universe.* Cambridge, Mass.: Harvard University Press, 2006.

Gleiser, Marcelo. *The Dancing Universe: From Creation Myths to the Big Bang.* New York: Plume, 1997.

Gold, Joshua I., and Michael N. Shadlen. "The Neural Basis of Decision Making." *Annual Review of Neuroscience* 30 (2007): 535–74.

Jastrow, Robert. *God and the Astronomers.* New York: Norton, 1992.

Linden, David J. *The Accidental Mind: How Brain Evolution Has Given Us Love, Memory, Dreams, and God.* Cambridge, Mass.: Harvard University Press, 2007.

Livio, Mario. *Is God a Mathematician?* New York: Simon and Schuster, 2009.

Pagels, Heinz R. *Perfect Symmetry: The Search for the Beginning of Time.* New York: Simon and Schuster, 1985.

Pinker, Steven. *The Blank Slate: The Modern Denial of Human Nature.* New York: Penguin, 2003.

——. *The Language Instinct: How the Mind Creates Language.* New York: Harper, 1994.

Roskies, Adina. "Neuroscientific Challenges to Free Will and Responsibility." *Trends in Cognitive Science* 10, no. 9 (2006): 419–23.

Roughgarden, Joan. *Evolution and Christian Faith: What Jesus and Darwin Have in Common; Reflections of an Evolutionary Biologist.* Washington, D.C.: Island Press, 2006.

Snow, C. P. *The Two Cultures.* Cambridge: Cambridge University Press, 1998.

5. In Defense of Religious Moderation

Bersani, Leo. *Homos.* Cambridge, Mass.: Harvard University Press, 1996.

Brooks, David. "The Catholic Boom." *New York Times,* May 25, 2007. http://select.nytimes.com/2007/05/25/opinion/25brooks.html?_r=1 (accessed January 31, 2010).

Dionne, E. J. *Souled Out: Reclaiming Faith and Politics After the Religious Right.* Princeton, N.J.: Princeton University Press, 2008.

Harris, Sam, and Andrew Sullivan. "Is Religion Built Upon Lies?" Debate available online at http://www.beliefnet.com/Faiths/Secular-Philosophies/Is-Religion-Built-Upon-Lies.aspx?p=1 (accessed on January 31, 2010).

Lacan, Jacques. *The Ethics of Psychoanalysis.* Translated by Dennis Porter. New York: Norton, 1997.

McGrath, Alister, and Joanna Collicutt McGrath. *The Dawkins Delusion: Atheist Fundamentalism and the Denial of the Divine.* Downers Grove, Ill.: IVP Books, 2007.

The Pew Forum on Religion and Public Life. http://pewforum.org/ (accessed May 21, 2010).

Robbins, Jeffrey W. *In Search of a Non-Dogmatic Theology.* Boulder, Colo.: Davies Group, 2004.

Rorty, Richard, and Gianni Vattimo. *The Future of Religion.* Edited by Santiago Zabala. New York: Columbia University Press, 2005.

Sullivan, Andrew. *The Conservative Soul: How We Lost It, How to Get It Back.* New York: HarperCollins, 2006.

Vattimo, Gianni, and René Girard. *Christianity, Truth, and Weakening Faith: A Dialogue.* Edited by Pierpaolo Antonello. Translated by William McCuaig. New York: Columbia University Press, 2010.

Wolfe, Alan. *One Nation After All: What Americans Really Think About God, Country, Family, Racism, Welfare, Immigration, Homosexuality, Work, the Right, the Left, and Each Other.* New York: Penguin, 1999.

——. *The Transformation of American Religion: How We Actually Live Our Faith.* New York: Free Press, 2003.

Index